THE
HUMBLE
ARGUMENT

THE
HUMBLE
ARGUMENT

Roy K. Humble

Problem Child

Dallas

Published in the United States of America.

ISBN: 978-0-9818181-3-9

CONTENTS

Part Three: Presenting Your Argument

Part Four: Improving Your Argument

ABOUT THIS BOOK

TO MY COLLEAGUES

This book exists because I have grown old and lack the vigor to continue translating the language of rhetoric textbooks into the language of my students. The ideas in this book are the basic ideas of argument, together with conventional advice for putting together a thoughtful college essay. My innovation is merely to strip from these ideas the terminology by which writing professors identify themselves as writing professors.

The placid countenance of the non-major should not be mistaken for comprehension. These students have merely learned that it's best to remain quiet as we wax on about commas and syllogisms and *Beowulf.* By using ordinary language, this book helps those uninitiated students to grasp the ideas of argument on their own. It helps them to put those ideas to good use, too, without having to raise their trembling hands and ask us to explain, for the thousandth time, what exactly we mean by "enthymeme."

The first section introduces the argumentative essay and

sound argumentative practices by comparison to inadequate versions of the same. The second section focuses on the process of building an inductive argument, moving from question to evidence to conclusion to presentation. The third section presents guidelines for constructing a solid but not particularly fancy college essay.

In the final section, I attempt to strengthen this working understanding of argument and the college essay by stepping gently in the direction of traditional terminology and rhetorical approaches. These chapters augment the inductive process from earlier chapters with deductive reasoning and more direct consideration of audience, but they are only an introduction so that others more ambitious than I might continue in that direction.

Colleagues, I agree that traditional rhetoric has for several dozen centuries required no help from the likes of me. Exordium is exordium is exordium — whatever else I might call it — and I do not suggest otherwise. This translation of mine is merely the consequence of my own failure to draw students into that finer vocabulary. If you have succeeded where I have failed, I salute you. However, if you too have struggled to make traditional rhetoric useful to your students, then perhaps this book will serve as a useful addition to your classroom, a bridge over which your students might travel more easily.

TO STUDENT WRITERS

Student writers, I don't imagine the preceding paragraphs mean much to you, but don't worry about that. The rest of the book is yours. It isn't much of a book, but that's okay, too. You don't need much of a book to learn how to write an effective college essay.

You do need some sensible guidelines, and you'll find those here. It's also a good idea to find someone who's better at writing than you are, someone who can help you apply these sensible guidelines and check your progress. A writing professor comes to mind.

The most important requirement, however, is simply that you write, and write a lot, so you can see for yourself what it means to put these guidelines into practice. Learning to write the college essay is like learning to French kiss. Reading about it will only take you so far. To learn how to actually do it, you have to actually do it, again and again. That's the main thing.

If you're reading this book because it can't be avoided — because it's part of a class you're taking — you need to pause now and give thanks for your writing assignments. They, more than anything, will help you to put these guidelines into practice. Embrace these assignments with gusto and the blind faith that they will do you some good. Ignore any anxiety you might feel. Repress unpleasant memories. If you're going to learn anything of lasting value in a writing class, the assignments will teach it to you.

Don't be afraid of struggling, either. You're learning new skills here, after all, and new skills do not come easily. Making mistakes will be an unavoidable and important part of the learning process. They are in fact evidence that you're getting somewhere. So just make your mistakes, correct them, and then move on to make more sophisticated errors. It's not that big of a deal.

When I was in second grade, I came running into the house one afternoon yelling for my mother and blubbering because I'd gotten a frowny face on a math test. We'd moved into long division without any warning, and I'd missed six out of ten problems. Mom was at an Amway meeting, as I recall, but my older sister Nadine was in the living room practicing for her interpretive dance recital. I told her about the frowny face.

"It's just math," she said, waving her arms to simulate the branches of a tree enlivened by a summer breeze. "*Anyone* can learn math."

It's the same story with argument and the college essay. It might *feel* overwhelming at first, particularly if these are new ideas for you, but it's just argument. It's just the college essay. You don't need any fancy books or websites or interactive DVDs. Just do the work in front of you. You'll get where you need to go.

Anyone can learn writing, and that includes you.

Part One

INTRODUCING THE COLLEGE ESSAY

You might think you know all about the college essay because you've written things in the past and your teachers called those things "essays." This section will show you why you might need to think again.

The college essay is an argument. It's not a report, nor a story, nor a reflection paper. It's also not the five-paragraph trainer-essay, which might be difficult news to bear. The college essay also requires a new kind of process that spends more time thinking about what to write than actually writing.

The two chapters in this section tell you, in so many words, to set aside any comfortable but inadequate ideas from the past and learn what it actually means to write a college essay of your own.

Chapter One

THE COLLEGE ESSAY IS AN ARGUMENT

You know the word "argument" because you've argued in the past. When you were young, for example, your mother told you to clean your room. You argued that it was just going to get messy again so there was no point in cleaning it and she should leave you alone for once in her life. When it comes to the college essay, many student writers continue to believe that a good argument is a loud argument. They write boldly. They make fun of their opponents. They ignore evidence that undercuts their positions.

Foolish student writers! That's not the kind of argument you make with a college essay. The college essay kind of argument must be thoughtful and honest and systematic. You start by asking a question that matters to you and your readers. After that, you consider any evidence you can find that's relevant to your question. Then, with the help of that evidence, you use your intelligence rather than a threatened ego to decide on the best available answer. Finally, and only after a lot of good thinking, you share your work with others — patiently, precisely, humbly, and in writing. No doors are to be slammed, no insults muttered under your breath.

You have also done this thoughtful kind of argument before now, though perhaps not in written form. When you chose a college to attend, for example, you started with a question. Oh no, you thought. What do I do now? You then considered your options, visited college websites, read brochures, talked to your equally confused friends, and arrived at a decision about how best to answer that question. And here you are.

When you bought your computer or your car or those amazing shoes — any purchase you actually thought about — you went through the same process of wondering which option was best, considering the evidence, and then making a decision. That's how a good argument works. With the college essay, you simply explain your decision in writing. Nothing could be easier.

Nothing could be easier, that is, except that "the college essay" is a label that many teachers apply to other papers that aren't really college essays because they aren't arguments. So before you get started with actual college essays, you'll need to tidy up your understanding of this term. You'll do that by first looking at the main ingredients required by an actual argument. After that, you'll compare actual college essays to other papers that may look like college essays but are not. Chapter Two continues this introduction by examining the process of writing college arguments and how it differs from the process of being a knucklehead.

A Brief Introduction to Argument

Argument is a field of study that's been around for thousands of years, so it's had plenty of time to become complicated and confusing. However, the basic ingredients of argument are fairly simple to understand. Here's what you need:

1. A question that matters to you and your readers.

2. Honest consideration of the relevant evidence.

3. A thoughtful decision about the best answer.

4. Careful presentation of your answer, your thinking, and the evidence.

If your essay includes all of these ingredients, it's probably an argument and thus a college essay. If any of these ingredients is missing, then it's probably not an argument and not a college essay. It's something that lives just down the street from the college essay, under a different name.

A Question that Matters

Arguments begin when people ask a question without a single clear answer or with several clear but competing answers, and they can't agree about which answer is best. Sometimes these are small questions: What movie should we see? Do these pants make my butt look big? Sometimes they're big questions:

Who should be the next president? Does wilderness have an intrinsic value? Will plaid sport coats ever be popular again?

If you and your sister agree that those pants really *do* make your butt look big, there's no argument. The question has one clear answer for both of you, so you have harmony — a sad harmony perhaps, a harmony that needs to eat better and exercise more, but harmony nonetheless. If, however, your sister thinks the pants make your butt look big while you think the pants have a slimming effect, then you have a question with more than one answer. You have disagreement, the potential for argument.

Besides having more than one reasonable answer, the question must also matter to both you and your audience. If my girlfriend and I disagree about how clean a bathroom needs to be, for example, we have the possibility for argument. It's actually more than a possibility. However, the disagreement has to matter to more than one party for an argument to actually happen. If my girlfriend decides to move out, the question of bathroom cleanliness doesn't matter to her anymore. I can leave beard stubble in the sink *for a week*, and there will be no argument.

If you don't care about politics, the question of who to vote for doesn't matter. *Whatever*, you think, and that's that. If your professor has no interest in wilderness — perhaps because she's teaching you about computer programming — then however passionate you might feel, the question of wilderness's intrinsic value doesn't matter enough for an argumentative essay.

RELEVANT EVIDENCE

Although your own experiences and observations might provide you with a good *hunch* about the best answer to an argumentative question, you need to set that hunch aside for the moment and consider as broad a range of evidence as time allows. That's because your personal views might not be as universal as they feel. The news report upon which you base your answer to the immigration situation might have left out a few facts. Your uncle Ken's opinion about global warming is probably not accepted scientific fact.

To arrive at the best answer to the question, you need to explore any evidence you can find, and you need to do so with an open mind, considering all available answers, consulting experts, and so on. You have to be willing to abandon your hunch if that's what the evidence suggests.

This isn't a matter of listing the pros and cons and going with the longer list. With argument, you need to look at the evidence more generally and search out patterns within it. You have to let the evidence determine what will be the best answer. With any college writing assignment, you're only given so much time, so when the time is up, you have to go with the best idea time allowed. Even so, don't be premature with your conclusions. The best ideas are rarely the easiest to find.

A THOUGHTFUL DECISION

With any good argumentative question, you won't find a right answer. You will instead find many plausible answers, and from these you will have to choose one. This will be a matter of opinion. The answer you choose will, in your opinion, be the best available answer to the question.

The word "opinion" is often used as a synonym for "guess," an idea that you think *might* be true even if you have little or no reason to think so. That's why we often add phrases like "that's just my opinion" or "I feel that" to our guesses. Why get into a fight over an idea we already doubt?

This is not the kind of opinion we're talking about with college essays. Your opinion should not be a guess but a thoughtful decision based on your consideration of the evidence. It should be an idea that you find reliable, and not just for yourself but for others, too. That's the kind of opinion required by the college essay.

CAREFUL PRESENTATION

By "careful," I do not mean "timid." If your essay is a good argument, you have considered a lot of relevant evidence, and that evidence has led you to a thoughtful decision about the best answer. You're in a good place, student writer. You should be confident about that evidence and your own thinking abilities. Just don't overdo it. Remember that while your answer to the question might be a good idea, it's not divinely inspired and it's not a fact. You still have to earn its acceptance with a careful presentation of what you think and why you think so

You should be respectful of those who disagree with you. They aren't idiots, probably. They just don't see things as clearly as you now do. You should also show your readers how your idea makes sense in the real world. You do that by offering actual evidence from the real world. Being careful means explaining your conclusions about the meaning of that evidence, too. And the best arguments will consider alternative answers and then explain why your answer is still better. That's the sort of care you should take when you explain and defend your opinion.

When you take the time to do all of the above, the essay you produce will be a college essay because it will be a fully formed argument.

WHAT THE COLLEGE ESSAY IS NOT

Throughout your formative years, your teachers called many things "essays." When your kind old fifth-grade teacher asked you to please write an essay about your summer "escapades," what she really meant was "write a story." When your cool junior high civics teacher told you write an essay about medical marijuana or hemp production or some other topic related to marijuana, what he meant was "write a report." Why did your teachers use "essay" for things that aren't arguments? They just did. Try not to dwell on it. Instead, take a few minutes to clean out some of these old misconceptions about what the college essay is and what it is not.

THE COLLEGE ESSAY IS NOT A REPORT

Reports are papers that give readers ideas and information about a topic. They're common in elementary and high school, and they persist less frequently as college assignments, too. A report requires you to inform yourself about a topic, which is a valuable skill, so that's a good assignment to give a larval student writer such as you were then. Reports aren't essays, however, because they focus only on a topic and not on a debatable question about that topic. More importantly, you never have to make any decisions about the meaning of the information you gather because a report doesn't present your own opinion as its main idea. It only presents the information.

It's fairly easy to write a perfectly acceptable report without thinking at all, as you probably know from experience. You might be old enough to remember opening an encyclopedia and copying down information "in your own words" without letting any of that information penetrate your brain. Or consider the times when you scoured the Internet for the first website that had any information on your topic. That didn't require much thought, did it? You can get away with that sort of non-thinking when it comes to information-laden reports, but it won't work with the college essay.

Here's a typical report-like piece of writing:

Pigdogs live in packs of up to six animals in established territories of up to one square mile. The territory tends to be bounded by natural features, such as rivers, or by man-made features such as interstate highways or fences. The territory includes a year-round source of water and a shaded area known as the "sty" where the pigdogs lounge as often as they are able and occasionally yip in their sleep.

Females bear one litter of up to eight pigpups every other year, except in times of drought. During times of drought, they typically band together with other females and fight off any rutting males.

The males are the hunters of the pack, though they tend to flee any animal that moves quickly, such as a rabbit. Often they come back to the pack bearing fast-food wrappers and Pepsi cups or road kill that is not too intimidating. They may also stalk fruits and vegetables, acting as if the plants were dangerous animals, and bring these spoils back to the sty with a great display of pride.

In this example, the author provides facts that inform you about the topic of "pigdogs." No question is raised. No answer serves as the main idea of the paper. What you have instead is raw information presented with some care. Thus we have a report. For this to become an essay, the author needs to answer a debatable question about the topic and then use relevant information about pigdogs as evidence to defend that answer.

Here's a short essay that asks the question, "What should the Department of Fish and Wildlife do about non-native species?" In this paper, the author uses the example of pigdogs to explain what he or she has decided is the best answer to that question:

Non-native species have a way of destroying the environments they invade, and that's why the Department of Fish and Wildlife must act more aggressively in its attempts to eradicate these species. A good illustration of failed eradication can be found in the case of the Norwegian pigdogs that have taken over large parts of California's Central Valley.

Pigdogs run in packs of five to eight animals over small territories (often defined by roads or irrigation ditches). They first arrived in California's Santa Clara region in 1911 as pets aboard the German freighter *Emilie*. Having been thrown overboard by the sailors during a drinking binge, the pigdogs swam to shore and quickly adapted to the surrounding environment, starting in Samuel County and moving southward.

Perhaps because they appear shy, or because of their odd habit of gathering roadside garbage, pigdogs have been considered harmless for decades. It was only five years ago that wildlife biologists realized that pigdogs had begun to crowd out native species such as raccoons and ground squirrels. Efforts to curb the spread of pigdogs by removing roadside garbage only resulted in pigdogs moving into farmers' fields and orchards where they began eating themselves into the population explosion that continues today.

If more aggressive eradication tactics — trapping, shooting, poisoning — had been taken earlier, pigdogs would not now be eating one-third of the annual nectarine crop, among other things.

This writer uses much of the same information about pigdogs as you find in the report, but the purpose for that evidence has changed. It's no longer just a collection of facts to inform us about a topic. In this essay, it has become evidence that helps to explain and defend the writer's answer to a question.

Stories, by the way, are really just reports, too. We call them stories or narratives because they report or narrate an event of some sort, often focusing on key actions and the characters who perform those actions. Because of that emphasis, they seem different from reports. And they're more interesting, usually — we enjoy a good story. However, they do not respond to a debatable question, and they do not present your own reasonable answer to that debatable question. What they do instead is present information about a topic — in this case, an event — so that readers will better understand that topic.

That makes them a type of report.

Paraphrasing is another type of report that sometimes looks like an essay. When paraphrasing, a writer might happen to report someone else's opinion, putting that idea into his or her own words. While this looks like an essay because of that other person's opinion, it remains a report because the paraphrased answer is not the writer's opinion. Instead, the writer is simply reporting the fact that someone *else* has an opinion.

In the college essay, you will regularly need to paraphrase the ideas of others. It's a good way to compress and include these ideas as you defend your own opinions. However, reporting someone else's opinion is no substitute for you figuring out your own answer to a good question.

THE COLLEGE ESSAY IS NOT A REFLECTION PAPER

Reflection papers typically respond to a question: What do you think about this? The writer must then generate some kind of answer to the question and put it in writing. Because of these qualities, the reflection paper does look something like a college essay. However, if we look more closely, the similarity starts to break down. Consider this short reflection paper:

> So what do I think about this article? One thing I learned was that writing is important. You have to be able to write in order to succeed in our society. People expect you to write well. If you can't express yourself well as a writer, then you will miss out on many important opportunities. I don't really agree that spelling should count as much as it does. That just turns everyone into spelling freaks, and what really matters isn't your

spelling but the ideas spelled out by your words, whether or not your words are spelled correctly.

Email was another thing that stood out for me in this article. That seemed so out of date. Nobody *emails*. Not like we did when it first came out when we were in *grade school*. Back then it was all about doing email because email was so new, but people don't email anymore. They text. The world changed, and someone forgot to tell this author. Some people still email, of course, but nobody I know except my *mother*.

One thing I'd like to know is whether writing will even exist once everyone has video phones because honestly....

You get the idea. It isn't pretty, but this short reflection paper does seem to include the elements of an argument, including a question, evidence, and answers. But look more closely at how this works. With a paper like this, the question — what do you think? — isn't an argumentative question because there's only one reasonable answer. Whatever the author says is the answer. You can't reasonably respond by telling that writer, "That's not what you think! You think email is awesome!"

This sort of paper considers evidence, too, but there's no guarantee that it will be thoughtful consideration. There's no need for thoughtfulness. Similarly, while the author does decide what he or she thinks, this is not a decision about what is the best answer to the question. This is simply a spilling of brain waves onto paper. The only real decision is when to turn off the brain faucet.

When it comes time for the presentation, the lack of focus is particularly noticeable. Without a clear question to debate, or thoughtful consideration of relevant evidence, or a decision about which is the best answer to a question, the paper becomes a mishmash of sentences that may or may not stick to one main idea. That kind of writing is clearly not the careful presentation of a single answer and its defense.

In college, the reflection paper is usually assigned to get you to read something. The assignment provides your professor with mild assurance that you did the reading, and perhaps that you also thought about what you read. The reflection paper is also assigned because it's so easy to grade. The professor only has to skim your work to make sure the paper stays on the right topic. This is useful, particularly if a loved one likes to complain that the professor never has any time for her because all he ever does is read papers "like a freaking readaholic." This ease of grading only underscores the point that reflection papers are not particularly thoughtful works.

Rants are a kind of unsolicited reflection paper. In a rant, the author adopts a general and often emotional position toward a topic and then lets loose a broad stream of invective toward the target of the rant. You can find plenty of this in the letters-to-the-editor section of the local newspaper or in "reader comments" to online news stories, or in blogs, where colorful writing leads to popularity, and popularity creates the illusion of credibility. People get worked up about the way "government" keeps interfering with their right to fire machine guns in their own backyards, or how dog owners never clean up their own dogs' poop — or whatever else — and they respond to the situation by typing rapidly. What comes out of those rapidly moving fingertips may feel coherent because it was written while in an angry mood, but it's really just a grumpy, rambling reflection paper about a topic or news story.

THE COLLEGE ESSAY IS NOT A FIVE-PARAGRAPH TRAINER-ESSAY

The five-paragraph trainer-essay is usually a report or a reflection paper rather than an actual college essay. This might offend some of you who have, in the past, earned high marks for these papers. However, the five-paragraph trainer-essay is only called an essay for the same reason that a training bra is called a bra, which is the same reason that toddler diapers are called "training pants" instead of "underpants-like diapers for kids who should be using toilets by now." These terms make you feel better about yourself as you go through these awkward and often embarrassing transitions.

The five-paragraph trainer-essay is primarily a template. An introductory paragraph presents a topic and a main idea about that topic: "This paper will look at the costs, the benefits, and the challenges of making your own ice cream." Each of three body paragraphs presents information about one subtopic of this topic, for example: "The costs include whole milk, salt, flavoring, and other costs that together are not that much more than the cost of store-bought ice cream." After you finish your three body paragraphs, a concluding paragraph summarizes your reflections and encourages readers to make their own ice cream. Into this template, you can insert any information you want as long as it's related to the same topic. If no opinions of your own are included, then the end result is a short report about that topic. If opinions work their way onto the page, you have a reflection paper.

The five-paragraph trainer-essay is popular in elementary

and high school because it's easy for teachers to teach and easy for students to learn. It's something a beginning student writer can accomplish almost from the start. The results are so much better than the usual chaos of adolescent minds, it's no wonder this template was a part of so many of your classes back in the day. However, the tidiness of the five-paragraph trainer-essay is not the same thing as thinking for yourself, much less writing an actual argument.

If you are able to present a real argument within just five paragraphs, then so be it. You will have then written a five-paragraph essay and not just a trainer-essay. When that happens, step back and admire the way it metaphorically illustrates your writerly evolution. There you stand, student writer, with one foot in your trainer-essay past and one foot in your college-essay present. Take a moment. Strike a pose. And then, for your own sake, say good-bye to the five-paragraph trainer-essay and continue to write the real thing — ignoring forever the number of paragraphs you compose.

THE COLLEGE ESSAY IS NOT A PERSONAL ESSAY

The English classroom is probably the only place where professors might ask you to write about yourself, and they do so not because they care that much about you (sorry) but because they want you to enjoy writing. Writing about yourself is usually easy and engaging and rewarding, so that makes sense. Your writing professors also want you to use writing to explore and examine your own experience in the world. That's what they do with writing, and they would like you to be as cool as they are.

While writing professors might have good reasons to ask you to write about yourself, they might also be giving you the wrong impression about you as a potential topic for the college essay. Your life is a topic that matters to you and the people who love you and the people who used to love you and now think a lot about revenge. Your life is not, however, a topic of study in your college classes — not directly. Any questions you raise about yourself will not be questions that matter to your professors. For that reason, no matter how thoroughly you consider the relevant evidence, no matter how thoughtfully you decide upon an answer, and no matter how artfully you present your argument in writing, the result will not be a college essay. It will be a personal essay.

You might be asking, Can I at least write about someone I know? Can I write about my cat? Can I write about my grandfather, who is super interesting, who was once attacked by wolves and fought them off with his bare fists? Yes, you can write about anyone you choose. Will that be a college essay? Probably not. Just as you will have a hard time finding a college class that focuses on you, you will also have a hard time finding a college class that includes a focus on your cat or your super-interesting grandfather. You might find a class that focuses on wolves, but I'd be careful about playing up that part about the bare fists.

And let's be honest about this, student writer, while these people you know do have lives of their own, you want to write about them because they're part of *your* life. The same goes for your favorite place to drink beer, for the time you climbed a modest but impressive-sounding mountain, for the way your iPod somehow knows what you're thinking before you do — that's still *you* we're talking about, so that's the personal essay, not the college essay.

That being said, your life does have a place in the college essay. In fact, your life has two places. First, your experiences have probably raised some questions that matter to you and others in a college classroom. You might have witnessed with your own eyes the effects of an oil spill on a beach you know. You might have wondered if there was any way to prevent the oil from coming ashore like that. That's a question you could ask in an essay for an environmental science or public policy class. I don't know if engineering students have to write essays, but if they do and if you're an engineering student, this could be used in an engineering class, too. You might have suffered job discrimination. You might have broken your leg in a car accident or dated a juggler. Many of your experiences will raise questions that matter to you and are relevant to one of your college classes, and those questions might lead you toward a good college essay. Your life probably won't be mentioned in the essay, but the essay will at least be connected to your life by its question.

A second place for your life to appear in the college essay is as illustration. Personal experiences rarely prove anything, but they often yield engaging anecdotes and observations that might help illustrate your ideas and make a personal connection with your readers. You might begin an essay with a brief memory of walking down an oil-contaminated beach, your feet covered with tar, tears streaming down your face, and so on, and then go from there to the more relevant question that your college essay will answer: What can be done to prevent this from happening again? You might recall your grandfather's fist-fight with wolves and then ask the question of whether reintroducing wolves to the American West is a sound management policy. There's not a lot of room for your life in the college essay, but this illustrative role offers some comfort for those who long to write about themselves. It's a niche you can fill, your own little cameo appearance in the essay.

At this point, you might be wondering about the collection of essays that was probably assigned as a textbook for your writing class. Many writing classes use these "college readers," and most of these readers are filled with personal essays, not college essays. What's the deal with that? The deal is that personal essays — and by that I mean *great* personal essays — are usually more interesting than arguments. For that reason, they often find their way into national magazines and remain popular long after those publications go out of business. When a publisher decides that the world really needs a new college reader, the publisher tends to use these same essays so that this new college reader will look interesting to writing professors. The result is yet another collection of mostly personal essays about shooting elephants, flinging starfish into the ocean, watching a kid jump into a lake, sitting in a jail cell, and so on.

If you didn't know any better, you might be tempted to skip over the sensible guidelines in this book and get right to the task of writing great personal essays. The thing about those essays, however, is that while they are easy and fun to read, they are difficult to write. For most of us, they are out of reach while we're in college, or while we're in graduate school, or while we're slogging through life teaching English composition for part-time wages at an underfunded and mismanaged community college in the middle of nowhere — hypothetically.

The more serious problem with even great personal essays, however, is that aside from a few young, untarnished English professors, your college professors aren't interested in reading personal essays. Your other professors want to see your answers to questions that are relevant to their classes. They want to see that you have considered evidence outside of your personal experience, and they want you to present your arguments clearly and concisely. They also have dozens of other papers to read besides yours, not to mention interminable faculty meetings, so they may become ill-tempered if you stray much from your assigned task in order to unravel the mysteries implicit in your recent trip to the grocery store.

THE COLLEGE ESSAY IS NOT EVEN A PERSUASIVE PAPER

The purpose of the persuasive paper is to persuade readers to agree with you. It's often assigned with a set of readings that examine a complex social issue by reducing all that complexity into a simple pro versus con, black versus white, yes versus no. The students then pick a side and write an essay that attempts to persuade others to join their team.

This looks just like an argument, doesn't it? You start with a question that can be answered reasonably in more than one way, such as pro or con. You have relevant evidence to consider in the set of readings. You have to decide your answer to the question. You have to carefully make your case so that you will get as many people from the pro team to join you and all the other cool people on the con team.

Although a persuasive paper will sometimes become an authentic college essay, it is more likely to be good advertising than good argument. The main problem is that the purpose of persuading tends to skew the presentation of your ideas and evidence. Even if you keep an open mind while looking at the relevant evidence, and even if you draw a sound conclusion from that evidence, the goal of persuasion encourages you to play up the evidence that supports your answer and play down or even ignore the evidence that does not. It encourages you to be bolder in your conclusions than the evidence really allows as a show of confidence. And for the truly crafty, the goal of persuasion encourages you to play upon your readers' fears or vanities rather than build a reasonable case for your ideas. Too often, the persuasive essay becomes an act of salesmanship because its success is measured by whether or not people buy the idea you're selling.

The goal of the college essay, on the other hand, is always to find and share the best available answer to a real, debatable question. The college essay will present that answer clearly and defend it with evidence. Persuasion might result from this, but persuasion is not the goal. Honesty is the goal. This is a small but important point to keep in mind. You don't have to win the college essay kind of argument.

THE COLLEGE ESSAY IS HARD WORK

College essays will almost never be as easy to write as reports or reflection papers or even persuasive papers. Those easier papers were a developmental stage in your life as a writer and thinker. You learned a lot from writing them, but now it's time for you to move on to more challenging work. The sooner you are able to accept this, the sooner you can advance to the next developmental stage — writing the college essay, as outlined in the chapters ahead.

Many student writers arrive at the college essay with the strong belief that this type of assignment will require nothing more than plugging information into templates or rattling off whatever comes to them — the same basic formula that's been working for them since they were pups.

I'm an excellent writer, the student writer says. I've always gotten A's in all my writing classes. Just tell me what you're looking for.

That kind of confidence is wonderful to see, but it makes the student writer deaf to my response. Find a good question, I say. Research the relevant evidence. Decide on the best answer to the question. Present your decision carefully. That's what I'm looking for.

I understand that, the student writer says. But what exactly does that look like — on paper? Just tell me that, and I'm set.

Unfortunately, it's not that simple. And here is where the challenge lies.

The college essay isn't defined by what it looks like on paper. It's defined by what it looks like in your brain. It's an idea that you figure out for yourself after considering relevant evidence. No two ideas are the same, so with each college essay you write, you have to find out for yourself what it's going to look like on paper.

That's why the college essay is hard work.

Chapter Two

THE COLLEGE ESSAY
IS A PROCESS

Student writers often think of the college essay as pages filled with words, as something they have made, something they can now hand in for a grade. In a way, they're right. The essay is a thing that they hand in for a grade. It's a bunch of words that they have put onto paper. It's something that professors write on and grade and hand back.

However, the college essay does not create itself. It's an end product, the result of something that student writers do. And if the essay is any good, the majority of work happens before any typing takes place. So while it makes some sense to think of the essay as a product, it makes more sense to think of it as a process, a set of steps that help student writers to first develop a good argument and afterward present that argument on paper.

This chapter begins with a look at some common and inadequate approaches to the writing process. You will thus be able to clean out any misconceptions and then replace them with a better, practical process for writing college essays.

START THINKING FOR YOURSELF

When I ask a new class full of writing students to explain their process for writing essays, they offer many types of responses. Three common responses are fairly benign and easy to eradicate. For these writers, the writing process is essentially a mystery, but one that they have conquered with reliable ritual. Here's a sample explanation:

> Whenever I have to write an essay, I sit in my room and turn off all the lights except for the computer monitor, which goes to a screen saver of traveling through the universe, like on *Star Trek*. I like to light a candle, too, to help me relax. Vanilla is a good scent. After that, I wait for an idea to come to me. Usually something comes to me after about five minutes. I never question what it is. I just go with it. I write and write until I get it all out and onto paper — or the computer. Then I stop. If there's time, I come back later to check spelling and stuff, but I almost never change anything.

Good luck with not changing anything, student writer.

A second common method is just as magical, but it's less overtly so. I call this process "composting":

> When I need to write an essay, the first thing I do is go to the library or Wikipedia and just read about it for like an hour. Sometimes I take longer, but only if I'm into it. Then I just write about whatever I've read. The information all kind of flows together onto the page. I go over it once to smooth things out, but if I spend more time than that, the process starts to break down.

Of course the process starts to break down, student writer. That's because it's not a process. It's just your subconscious mind doing its thing.

A third common approach depends less on magical ritual and the subconscious mind and more on other people. This isn't exactly plagiarism, but it does rely on something other than your own ability to think. Here's an example:

> Whenever I have a paper assignment, my mother and I like to sit down and talk things through, and she lets me know when I have something that seems like it would be a good paper. Then I go off and write it on my own. That might take an hour. Then we work on revising it together. She was a teacher for many years, so she knows about how to write papers. She's the one who taught me that an essay should have three supporting paragraphs, which I still think is the best way to do it. None of my previous teachers have had any problems with it. In fact, I have always gotten excellent grades in all my English classes UNTIL THIS TERM. I used to enjoy writing — A LOT.

Sorry for ruining your life, student writer!

What you see in these three examples is an abdication of the writers' responsibility to think for themselves. Instead, they let their moms or their subconscious minds or mysterious forces of the universe do the thinking for them. They seem to believe that the writing process is more powerful than the writer, and thus that they have no choice but to follow whatever process they've fallen into. However, writing the college essay is just a set of actions that can be learned and improved upon. No magic is required. Mothers are optional. This process might feel awkward at first, especially if you set aside something comfortable like vanilla-scented candles, but awkward is normal. When it comes to learning new things, awkward is a good sign that you're getting somewhere.

The more you practice a new process, the less awkward it becomes, until eventually you can look back at your former process and smile nostalgically at what a goofball you used to be. You've done this a hundred times before with a hundred other new skills. It's not like you left the womb knowing how to tie your shoes or drive a car or find a moderately priced Thai restaurant. Writing the college essay can be a fairly complex process, so learning how to do it might take some time, but it's still just something you do, a process you can learn to do for yourself. It's not bigger than you are. It's *nothing* compared to something really difficult like ballroom dancing.

At some dark moment in your past, some teacher might have told you that you were just a bad writer, as if bad writing was a rash, and you had it, and it wasn't going to get better. If you took that teacher's diagnosis seriously, you might now cling even harder to any ritual that works for you. But here's the real story with an incident like that: The teacher was just a bad teacher. You may not have had the skills you needed to be an effective writer *at the time*, but your teacher was blaming you for his or her failure to teach you how to improve. What a rotten teacher! I'm sorry for your terrible luck.

The fact is that writing is not a genetic condition. People may grow up to be more or less comfortable in their ability to use written language, just as they may grow up to be more or less comfortable in their ability to remain upright on a skateboard. However, in the same way that anyone can learn how to skateboard, anyone can learn how to write the college essay. All you have to do is start out simply and get better with practice. You might not become a professional writer, but with enough practice, you *can* become competent and comfortable with this process.

DON'T BE A KNUCKLEHEAD

While any of those three not-so-thoughtful student explanations of the writing process might be painful for student writers to leave behind, their inherent weaknesses are easy to understand and make fun of. It doesn't take long for student writers to see this for themselves and put aside these old ways.

A fourth common and inadequate process is related to the persuasive paper you read about in Chapter One. This process is more difficult for student writers to leave behind because it looks so much like the process of writing a good argument. Here's one student's explanation:

> The way I write a paper is to figure out what I want to say and then look for evidence that will support it. I usually know what I want to say right away. Ideas just come to me like that. I'm not opinionated, but I have a lot of good ideas. If I can find enough evidence to support my idea, then I just start writing and put it all in the paper. If I can't find enough evidence, then either I start over with a different idea (hardly ever) or I use common knowledge to explain what I mean.

This explanation reminds me of waiting for my first swim lesson to begin, hanging out in the wading pool with all the other Pollywogs. I was intensely afraid of the big pool, so to convince my mother that I didn't need swim lessons, I laid down in the wading pool and used my arms to move around. "Mom!" I yelled. "Look! I can swim! I don't need lessons!" There was a part of me that really wanted to believe it, too. But Mom barely looked up from her magazine. "That ain't swimming, Roy," she said. "That's just being a knucklehead." The other mothers laughed. I felt like an idiot, but Mom did have a point.

It's the same point I make to students when they present this particular process for writing the college essay. That ain't the college essay, student writer. That's just being a knucklehead. Yes, you've got an opinion for a main idea, and yes, you've found the evidence to back it up, but it's not a college essay because you've reversed the two central steps of the argumentative process.

As you saw in Chapter One, a good argument has four main ingredients. The process for writing a good argument has four main steps to match those ingredients:

1. Ask a good question.

2. Consider relevant evidence.

3. Decide on the best answer.

4. Carefully present your answer.

When you write like a knucklehead, you start with a question and end by presenting your answer, so the knucklehead essay *looks* like an argument. However, knuckleheads reverse the order of steps 2 and 3. Instead of letting evidence lead them to the best available answer, knuckleheads use an answer — any answer — to gather up supporting evidence and get rid of contradictory evidence.

The knucklehead writing process looks like this:

1. Ask a question (usually one that's easy to answer).

2. Decide on an answer (probably a hunch).

3. Look for evidence to defend that answer.

4. Present the answer and evidence.

This is the writing process of conspiracy theorists. They answer a question with a suspicion: The mob assassinated John Kennedy. The September 11th attacks were an inside job. Barack Obama wasn't born in America. Then they use that suspicion to judge whether evidence is credible or not. If a piece of evidence defends their suspicion, they say it's credible evidence. Anything else is just part of the conspiracy and is rejected. Knuckleheads then use the evidence they accept to confirm that their suspicion is a good idea.

It's possible, of course, that a suspicion is also true. It's thus possible that a knucklehead's suspicion could become the main idea of a pretty good essay. However, that will only be an accidental outcome. Knuckleheads won't actually know whether a suspicion is the best available answer to a question because they won't have tested that idea with evidence. Instead, they'll have tested the evidence with their idea. They haven't been open to other plausible, and possibly better, answers to the question. The idea they started with — good or bad — has only become a more strongly held prejudice.

Thinking for yourself does not mean accepting just any idea. It means being thoughtful for yourself. It means using evidence to find the best available ideas, and by testing your ideas to make sure they're worth holding onto.

HOW TO WRITE THE COLLEGE ESSAY

Learning how to write the college essay may not be a lot of fun at first. I hated swim lessons — and not just that first summer, either, but for the next two summers until I finally graduated from Pollywogs. It might be that kind of a struggle for you. Or you might be like my sister Nadine, who passed Pollywogs on her first attempt. You might have a strong aptitude for using words. You might have had a high school teacher who expected you to think for yourself and use evidence to test your ideas. Don't worry about how quickly you succeed with this process. The point is to push ahead, whether or not it comes easily, so that with practice you get better. Here's how the process breaks down into the four main steps that were mentioned above, using a hard-hitting local news story as an illustration of how this works.

STEP 1: ASK A GOOD QUESTION

A good question has three main qualities. It should be debatable, it should be answerable, and it should matter to you and your readers.

If a question can only be answered in one way — with a fact or an idea that's so widely accepted that it might as well be a fact — then the paper you will write will be a report that explains that fact rather than an essay that defends your own opinion. If you ask *how* milk is pasteurized, for example, there's only one answer, so a paper that explains that idea will be a report. If you ask whether or not milk *should* be pasteurized, you will quickly learn that a fierce debate exists over the value of pasteurization. Because more than one credible answer exists, your essay can enter that debate and propose an opinion about the best answer.

A good question is also answerable. That means there must be sufficient evidence with which you can decide on the best possible answer. When there's little or no evidence to consider, your answer is just guesswork and has little or no value for you or your readers. You might ask, for example, what the world would be like now if Louis Pasteur hadn't invented pasteurization. That's an interesting question, perhaps, but there's no evidence available with which to answer it. All you can do is speculate. Your speculation might be interesting — and could form the basis for an unsuccessful science fiction novel — but it won't be sufficient evidence for a college essay.

A good question will also be one that matters to you and your readers. With the college essay, it is possible to get away with a question that doesn't *really* matter to you or your reader (the professor). You may not care about pasteurization, for example, but if a professor assigns you the task of answering a question about its appropriate use within developing nations, you can still write an argument because the class itself matters. Or, to turn it around, *you* might raise a question that you like about whether organic juices should be pasteurized. As long as the question has more than one possible answer, and as long as the question is relevant to the assignment, it doesn't matter whether your professor cares about that question personally. Part of what student writers do in college is practice argument for later use, so it doesn't always have to be personal.

As much as you can, however, you should look for a question that really does matter to you. It makes the entire process more enjoyable and rewarding. Your professors assign essays so that you will learn something new and hopefully learn how to examine issues like they would — as historians or psychologists or biologists. So try to have some fun with that. Use the assignment as an opportunity to satisfy some small part of your ever-expanding curiosity. Accept your assignments as they are intended and you will find they offer more rewards than just a grade.

Early in the term, I like to assign students to read an article from the front page of a local newspaper and develop an essay in response to that article. Suppose, for example, that your city council votes to impose an annual $50 tax on raising chickens within the city limits. Owners of chickens don't like the tax, but the city council says the tax is needed to pay for someone to oversee chicken-raising operations, and that the only alternative would be to ban chickens entirely.

With an article like this, you might start your essay by asking any of several questions. For example, you might ask what happened. That's probably not a good question because there seems to be general agreement about what happened: The city council decided to impose a tax on chickens. If your essay attempted to answer that question, it would look a lot like the newspaper article — a collection of information, a report rather than an essay. The same would be true of other, more focused questions: How will the tax money be used? When does the tax go into effect? How many chickens live within the city limits? These probably aren't good questions because they each seem to point toward one generally agreed-upon answer.

A good question is one that can be answered with more than one credible answer. For example, you might ask if chickens are really a problem. The city councillors think they are. The chicken owners disagree. The question is thus debatable, so you can join the debate by adopting that question for your essay. As long as evidence is available to help make you a decision, this question could be the start of an essay.

You should do some light research to find out if the question you have in mind really is a question, but don't spend a lot of time gathering evidence yet. That comes later in the process. For now, it's enough to confirm that your question is debatable and answerable. If you find that it's not a good question, be adult about it and try again.

STEP 2: CONSIDER THE EVIDENCE

As you start out, you might have an answer in mind for your question. If so, ignore it. Treat that answer like the annoying musician friend who's been staying in your apartment for the last three weeks to "cheer you up" and shows no signs of leaving. Don't do anything to encourage it. You need to keep an open mind at this point, and that means setting aside any hunches and focusing just on the evidence. Your question will be a better guide as you gather and consider evidence. A hunch tends to focus your attention on evidence that's relevant to that idea, but a question lets in all sorts of evidence for consideration. The more evidence you consider, the more thoughtful your answer is likely to become.

With the question of whether chickens are really a problem, you might look for evidence in other newspaper articles. Something like a chicken tax doesn't make it onto a city council agenda without complaints. Find those complaints. What do the complainers have against chickens? How have the chicken owners responded? If you can't find anything more about chickens in your city newspaper, then look elsewhere. Your city is nothing special. If chickens have been debated in your city, they've been debated in other cities. To see how others might have answered this question in the past, you can look for editorials and letters to the editor.

To dig a little deeper, you might read the actual transcript of the city council meeting to examine the evidence that was reported in the newspaper. Many cities put recordings of their meetings online now. You can listen to the full meeting. That would be fun. In some cases, experts might have already asked the same question and put a lot of time into figuring out good answers. You can examine their answers and reasoning and see how they hold up in your situation.

You might also talk to others who know more than you. With most college assignments, you can talk to your professor to get a better understanding of an issue and find some guidance about where to look for information. This is particularly useful if you do some initial research and don't find much of anything. Reference librarians in your campus library are good resources, too. Or you may know someone whose job is related to your topic — your family doctor, your lawyer brother-in-law, the retired chicken inspector who moved into the apartment downstairs. Call your city councillor, who is a politician and therefore loves to talk. These local experts can all point you toward good, real-world information.

As a student, it's unlikely that you can do any meaningful, firsthand research. That will come later when you become so overeducated that the only way you can afford food and the Laundromat is by securing federal research grants. Even so, many student writers can't resist the urge to poll their friends to find out what they think. Those friends are good at keeping you from feeling lonely, but take a good, honest look at them. They aren't experts when it comes to chickens, city ordinances, public policy, or any other topic. They may give you a few more ideas to consider, but they almost certainly won't give you useful evidence. Don't tell them that, of course, but it's true.

This brings us back to the need for a good question. Once you start digging for evidence, you will quickly learn that it's not enough to just have a topic. The world is a complicated place, and even an apparently simple topic — chickens, for example — will expand outward in a hundred directions. Many student writers are skeptical of this. We're talking about chickens, they say. How complicated are chickens?

Foolish student writers! The proposed chicken tax in your city could be the tip of a devious plot by giant chicken farms to put the squeeze on locally produced poultry. It could be a skirmish in a broader class war. It could be a sign of a dramatic demographic shift in your community. Sometimes a chicken is just a chicken, of course, but sometimes a chicken is much more than that. That's why you follow a question instead of an answer. You have to let as much evidence as possible into your brain so that the evidence will take you wherever you need to go.

STEP 3: DECIDE ON THE BEST ANSWER

At some point, even with a topic as engaging and complex as chickens, you will run out of time for gathering and considering relevant evidence. When that happens, you have to decide how to answer your question. Your decision should be based on two things: your evidence and your honesty. Regarding the raising of chickens within city limits, you might not be too personally invested in the answer. That will make it easier for you to be honest about what the evidence tells you. However, if you're writing about something that matters a lot to you, and if it's something you've thought about for some time, and if the evidence is now pulling you toward an answer you didn't expect and don't like, honesty can be a challenge. Be honest anyway. Don't be a knucklehead.

Your answer needs to be precise, too. Until you define your answer precisely, you've only *kind of* decided what you think. A vague answer is really just a cluster of potential answers. To answer a question clearly, you need to define the idea clearly. For that, you need to translate the idea into words so that you can tinker with those words and make the idea better. Suppose, for example, that the evidence leads you to this answer:

> All chickens should be banned from within the city limits because they are noisy.

That seems reasonable enough, given the evidence at hand. You found plenty of real-world information to confirm that chickens really are noisy. Roosters are the noisiest, but the incessant clucking of the hens can be just as irritating. So say the people who live near the chickens.

But it's not just the noise that bothers the neighbors. It's also the smell. Chickens, it turns out, have poor bathroom habits. This leads to a strong smell that hovers over the neighborhood like smog. That's a part of the answer, too, so you can improve your answer by including that fact in your reasoning:

> All chickens should be banned from within the city limits because they are noisy and because they stink up the entire neighborhood.

That's better. It relies on a broader range of evidence. However, now you remember the article you read about the couple who own a breed of chickens that are mute and can be trained to relieve themselves in kitty litter. That information undercuts your reasons for banning chickens.

If you were still in high school, you would simply ignore these quiet, sweet-smelling chickens and pretend that your idea is invincible. Because you are in college, however, you decide to revise your answer so that it more honestly conforms to the more complex evidence you have gathered and considered:

> Chickens should be banned from within the city limits if they are noisy or if they stink up the neighborhood.

This is better. This sentence defines the boundaries of your answer more precisely. It's an idea you can more honestly defend, too, because it's a more honest idea. It will work well as the main idea of an essay. The answer still isn't perfect. It raises questions about implementation of that ordinance: What does it mean to be noisy? What does it mean to stink? Who will judge whether a flock of chickens is noisy or stinky? But that's a good sign, believe it or not. It means that you are moving into the complexity and complications of reality. Good for you.

STEP 4: CAREFULLY PRESENT YOUR ANSWER

Now, at last, it's time to share your thinking with others by presenting this answer as the main idea of an essay. This step in the process typically breaks down into three stages: planning, drafting, and revising.

Planning: To effectively explain and defend a complex main idea, you need to lay out your thinking in detail and present readers with plenty of evidence. The more clearly you organize your evidence into meaningful patterns, the more likely it is that your readers will see how all the information works together to explain and defend your main idea.

If my former girlfriend had one fault that really got on my nerves, it was the way she moved from point to point to point in some kind of free-association mental universe and then expected me to understand how it all made sense. When I objected, she became furious. "*You're* Mr. English Teacher," she used to say, as if that was an insult. "*You* tell me what my thesis is." I wish I had just told her what I was thinking: "I could — if you'd ever learn how to organize your evidence!" That's a snappier comeback in my mind than it is on paper.

My point, though, is that when someone throws a lot of disorganized information at you, you become confused. You don't see what all the evidence adds up to — if anything — and you gradually stop listening. To keep this from happening to your readers, you need to carefully inventory all the pieces of the evidence you plan to include in your essay and then arrange them according to an appropriate pattern.

One excellent tool to help you with this is a topic sentence outline. For each paragraph that you plan to write, summarize the purpose of that paragraph in a single, complete sentence. You then arrange those sentences so that the order of presentation makes sense. It might be chronological, for example, or it might move from most to least important idea.

When confronted with the suggestion of a topic sentence

outline, student writers will sometimes tell me, I never outline an essay. I just write from a mental outline. With a simple, short paper, that might work. Your mind might be large enough to do this. With a more complex paper, it probably won't work. To be sure you're making sense, take five minutes and briefly outline the information that helps to explain your main idea. Five minutes! It takes less time than flossing your teeth, and it won't make your gums bleed.

Drafting: This is where you put onto paper the actual words that will transfer an idea from your brain into the brains of your readers. Some writers can draft entire essays in their heads and then type them out as final drafts. These writers are so rare, however, that the federal government pays scientists to study them. I'm serious. If nobody's studying you, then you're probably not one of these writers. For you, there will be more than one draft.

A good way to start is to draft just the body of your essay. Student writers get way too hung up achieving the perfect opening line. To write the perfect opening line, or just an okay opening, you need to know what's in the body of the essay. A better starting point, then, is the body of the essay. So write a full paragraph for each point in your topic sentence outline. If you have to expand more important or complex points into multiple paragraphs, then do so. Another option is to write a quick, brief draft of the body and then expand upon and revise that draft until you remove the ineffective and irrelevant bits of information and include enough of the right stuff. The end result should be a set of paragraphs that all work together to present and defend one main idea. Once the body is done, drafting a good opening and closing is much easier.

Drafting often leads you to unexpected discoveries about your topic, your question, your idea, or yourself. Drafting relies on the subconscious mind to gather up the right words, and the subconscious mind, once activated, is creative and unpredictable. You might discover that you need to go back to your question and take another look at what the evidence really says. You might notice a new wrinkle in the evidence, and that might lead you to an even better main idea. You might also see that a big chunk of evidence isn't actually relevant to your particular question. You might have to junk it. You might have to go back to an earlier step in the process. You might need to reorganize your essay. If drafting shows you that you have to make changes, then make changes. Don't fall too deeply in love with what you've written.

Revising: This word might be used to describe any point at which you go back to an earlier step in the process and improve your idea, your evidence, your organization, or your draft. Revising in its broadest sense means "re-seeing." I have no quarrel with that broad use of the word, but that's not how it's used here. For our purposes, revision is only a matter of stepping back from your draft to polish it up for your audience.

You might introduce your question more colorfully in the opening, for example, or add or subtract bits of evidence to more efficiently defend your answer to the question. You might add a rebuttal to any of the other possible answers that you don't like as much as your own. In polishing your essay, you might even stumble upon a better answer to the question and thus face more drastic changes. If so, you know what you have to do about that.

Revision includes some focus on the mechanics of the essay, but save most of that until after you are confident of your answer and its argument. You don't want to spend time worrying about how to spell "accommodate" or where to put a comma when that whole paragraph needs to be eradicated from the essay. You also don't want to lock in weak or irrelevant paragraphs of evidence by polishing up the punctuation. After you invest a lot of time in polishing garbage, the garbage starts to look pretty good. But it's still garbage.

Feedback is an important part of revision. Because your essay is trying to take an idea from your brain and put it into the brain of another human, it helps to try the essay out on other humans, such as your professor, an editing group, a smart friend, and so on. This helps you check to see if the idea transfers successfully to other brains. One good thing about my former girlfriend was that she never had a problem telling me what she thought of something I'd written or said. That's the kind of feedback you should look for — feedback that isn't worried about your feelings. Don't ask people if they like your essay. That doesn't matter, and anyway, most of them will say that they like it so that you will leave them alone. Instead, ask them what they think your main idea is. If they can tell you, and if it *is* your main idea, then you've written a good essay because the main idea transferred successfully to their brains.

Student writers sometimes find it difficult to open up to feedback. They think that criticism of something they've written is criticism of their intelligence or personality. But it's not like that. What you've written is just that — something you've written. It's not you. It's not your intelligence. It's not a price tag on which is stamped your value to the world. And listen, even if the essay's great, it's not as good as your writing will be later on. It's just an artifact of where you are right now as a writer. If you can accept that your essay is just this thing you did, like the plastic ice scraper you made in eighth-grade shop class — which by the way was a pretty decent ice scraper — it's easier to take and benefit from the feedback.

This stage is over when the entire process is over — when you give your essay to its readers.

THE WRITING PROCESS FOR YOU

In the end, and in seeming contradiction to the start of this chapter, you *will* have to discover a writing process that works specifically for you. This is the work of your brain, after all, and no two brains are alike. Brains, in this regard, are like snowflakes.

You should start with the four-step process of finding a good question, considering relevant evidence, deciding on an answer, and presenting your answer to others. This is how argument works. It's been working this way for thousands of years, and there's no reason to think that will change in your lifetime. However, as you get comfortable with this process, you should adapt and refine it so that it works best for your particular situation and habits.

You might find that the hardest step for you is coming up with a good question, and that talking to your friends — regardless of how I've trashed them in this chapter — is a great help. So be it. Good for you. Adapt the process to include them if that's what it takes to get started. You might find that having your own special writing place is important, or that noise levels are a factor. You might need music or complete silence. You might need to turn off the television. It's good to figure these things out. Respect those discoveries and revise your writing process to include those conditions and precautions.

Some writers have turned to opium or grain alcohol to get started. That can get you started, all right, but it can also get you into the county jail for the weekend, followed by twelve to fifteen Sunday mornings of picking up trash in an orange vest. So be careful with your writing process. Don't risk too much.

If you try to use this four-step process and it doesn't go anywhere, don't panic. Above all, don't go back to any not-so-thoughtful processes from the past. Instead, talk to your writing professor. Most writing professors collect tricks for jump-starting writers at various stages of the writing process. If you don't have a writing professor, you can always search the Internet with these key phrases: "writing arguments" or "the writing process." A lot of what you find will be junk, of course, but you might also find just the right trick to get started.

Part Two

DEVELOPING YOUR ARGUMENT

Writing the college essay is more work than just putting words onto paper. Those words translate an idea from your mind into written form so that readers can take what you've written and translate it back into an idea in their minds.

The most important work of writing, then, happens before you do any writing at all. It happens as you develop your argument, as you build an idea that's worthy of translation into words on paper.

In the three chapters of this section, you'll look at the three main steps that go into building a good argument: asking a good question, considering the evidence, and deciding on the best available answer.

Chapter Three

ASK A GOOD
QUESTION

You begin the writing process with a question because the college essay — like argumentation and the human experience — is a process of discovery. A question helps you explore a wide range of evidence, consider many possible answers, and then arrive at the best answer you can find. It's hard to discover anything if you start with an idea you already have in mind. That's like sitting on your couch and planning a trip to the living room. You're already there, my friend. A good question, on the other hand, pushes you out the front door of what you already know and helps you discover a bigger neighborhood.

Finding a good question can be tricky, though. It has to be a question that matters to you and your readers. This can be especially challenging when you're assigned a topic about which you know little or nothing — which is exactly the sort of topic you're likely to be assigned, of course, this being college and all. Your question should also be a real question. That means the answer is debatable, but also that the question can be answered, reasonably, with evidence.

In this chapter, you'll take a look at how to find a good question, and then at how to make sure it really is a question. The chapter ends with a look at the single most important thing you can do to write a successful college essay.

FIND A QUESTION THAT MATTERS

When you're writing papers for actual college classes, your professors often give you questions that matter — to them, anyway. Does an assigned question matter to you? Whether it does or not, there's a good chance you'll answer it anyway because the grade matters to you. However, you can make the process of writing about an assigned question more engaging with a simple leap of faith.

Assume that your professor knows what he or she is doing by assigning this question. Even though you don't know enough about an assigned topic to care about it, your professor does, and your professor probably assigned this question so that you will discover something in this new topic that's worth writing about. If you *choose* to care about an assigned question, you'll often be rewarded with unexpected satisfaction.

What's more difficult is when your professor assigns a broad topic and then tells you to find a question of your own. I used to assign Shakespeare plays as topics, and the students would complain about this assignment for two reasons. Either they saw no relevance at all between their lives and the topic ("How is *Hamlet* going to help me become a better electrical engineer?") or they had already spent more time than they wanted with the topic ("But I already did *Macbeth* back in high school!")

Shakespeare is boring, they concluded, and I responded with the same thing my mother told me when I complained of boredom: Boring is as boring does. I'm not entirely sure what she meant by that. My mother said a lot of odd and sometimes hurtful things. However, what I've taken it to mean is that boredom isn't ever the problem. It's just a symptom. So if you're bored by a topic — according to my mother, anyway, I think — you haven't dug deeply enough into its complexities or made sufficient use of your imagination.

Fortunately, getting beneath the surface of a boring topic isn't that hard to do. In fact, there are some easy tricks to help you explore a dull topic just enough to find a question that interests you. Once you have a question that matters to you, even a little, the rest of the writing process becomes much more engaging and rewarding.

I'll show you a few techniques that can help you to find a good question within a difficult topic. The topic I'll use will be "holidays," which at the moment seems both irrelevant and boring. No single technique works for everyone, but one of these will likely work for you. If none of them works, then talk to your writing professor. There are many other tricks out there, and your professor had to study them in graduate school.

FREEWRITING

This technique requires you to write without ceasing for a set period of time — at least ten or fifteen minutes, and ideally more than that. There's no format to follow, no main idea to explain, and no commas to worry about because this is not your rough draft. With freewriting, you use the act of writing itself to draw ideas out from their hiding places in your brain and into the open.

The trick here is to keep going long enough to exhaust all the easy, superficial ideas. Writing is thinking, after all, so forcing yourself to write means forcing your brain to come up with ideas. Once the easy ideas are out of the way, you begin to see the sorts of things your subconscious mind has been working on beneath that mild-mannered exterior of yours.

For the college essay, your goal will be to find a narrow slice of your larger topic and within that slice a particular question that is debatable, answerable, and engaging. You need something that makes you mad or curious, something that you'd like to know more about. Here's an example of some actual freewriting from a while back:

> Holidays stink. I hate having to go to my sister's house. The whole stupid deal. We're all supposed to act like we love each other. Like we're this great family. Like we weren't practically KILLING each other every second of the day while we were growing up. Nadine used to sit on my belly and give me the typewriter treatment. I'm six years old and I have bruises all over my chest from her typing on me, and then the one time I barely tap her on the head, Mom's all over me. Girls are fragile! Girls are fragile! My CHEST was fragile! I was six! Even now Mom's way too in love

with Nadine and Larry and their kids and all the JUNK they have, how nice all their THINGS are. There's no way we'll ever have Christmas or ANY- THING at my place because one, it's just me now — I don't have the wife and kids or even the girlfriend anymore so I don't count — and two, it's just an apartment — and three, they were crazy about Denise and still yell at me for "letting her go." Hello? Who let go of whom? It doesn't matter! But it's like you have to be married, you have to have kids, you have to have your own house to count with these people. That's who holidays are designed for, people with families. People with THINGS. I can't think of a holiday that's designed for me, for someone who's alone and depressed. Not that I'm depressed. I am NOT depressed. I LIKE my solitude. Still, it's no wonder so many people do harm to themselves over the holidays. Spending the holidays in some little dump of an apartment. Holidays aren't designed for people who live in apartments. There should be a Lonely Guy Apartment Day or something. Something for normal people.

This is a rambling collection of ideas, a venting of sorts, and certainly not an example of good writing or even an accurate snapshot of where I'm at emotionally anymore. Even so, the list does offer a few possibilities that might lead to a good question. There's the connection between holidays and suicide, for example. That's not a new observation, I suppose, but perhaps the connection to apartments is new. Do apartment dwellers have a higher holiday suicide rate than home owners? If so, why? That's something that matters to me, so if it's also a real question, it could be a good question for an essay.

If I really want to poke at my wounds, I could take a closer look at why I hate my apartment. Do I accept the idea that apartments are inferior even as I condemn it? And although the connection of materialism and the holidays has been done before, I'm interested in the question about whether people value family mostly as a kind of possession.

Again, the purpose isn't to figure out the main idea of an essay. That comes later in the process. The purpose for now is to explore the possibilities of this topic and find a question that matters to me. Even in this short bit of freewriting about holidays, several questions emerge that probably matter to me, and they will be useful in the next step of the writing process if they prove to be actual questions.

REPORTERS' QUESTIONS

When I was in junior high school, my dream was to become a famous reporter. That didn't work out, obviously, but my two trimesters on the *Spartan Spectrum* did teach me "the 5 Ws and 1 H," six questions that any good journalist will ask to explore a topic: Who? What? When? Where? Why? and How?

The reporters' questions are usually more helpful after you've moved from a general topic — "holidays" — to a narrower subtopic. They help you explore and understand the specifics of that subtopic, and those specifics help you find good questions. Below are brief descriptions of how each question works, with examples linked to a holiday subtopic, "the problem with handmade gifts."

Who? These are the subjects that are doing something or are having something done to them. So who is doing something? To whom is it being done? Who else is affected? These actors might be human, or they might also be broader forces at work (unemployment, inflation) or groups (the NRA, unruly schoolchildren) or nations or ideas — anything that might do something, cause something to happen, or be affected. With this subtopic, the question could generate these answers:

my mother

Nadine and Larry

people with too much time on their hands

people who don't have to work for a living

me, the victim

people who see handmade as "real" and store-bought as "fake"

outdated cultural values? thriftiness?

What? This question looks at events and actions from the past, present, and future. These might be physical, observable events or internal, unobservable events. Think about change with this question. What changed? What is changing? What is likely to change? One technique here is to take each of the answers to "Who?" and look for the verb that goes with each noun. What does each do? What is done to each?

Here are some possible answers to this question:

Mom gives me a quilt every Christmas.

I put the quilt in my storage unit with the 25 other quilts I don't use.

I give Mom a nice sweater or kitchen appliance, which she takes to Walmart and exchanges for more quilting supplies.

Nadine gives me sweatshirts with pictures of her kids on them.

Larry gave me a BIRD HOUSE. Anybody home? I live in an apartment!

I can't just throw their gifts away because they're "handmade."

I can't exchange them for something I'd like.

They get so superior about it, too.

Some stupid cultural value makes handmade gifts good even if they're totally useless to me, even if they're insulting to me.

The same cultural value makes my useful and thoughtful gifts seem inferior to their junk.

When? This question might ask about a specific time or date. It might also consider the set of conditions that must be present for an event to happen, like the circumstances that must be present for the stock market to crash.

Here are some answers with the current topic:

Christmas season

Christmas morning

all year (sewing)

December 26 (trip to storage unit)

this century (how many people have the time to make stuff anymore?)

past centuries (when everybody made everything for themselves)

rise of consumerism (Is the valuing of handmade stuff a reaction to the rise of store-bought stuff? When most people had to make stuff, wasn't store-bought stuff preferred?)

Where? This question might look at actual physical locations or general cultural situations in which an event might take place. You can start with physical locations, but it's good to use your imagination here.

With this topic, you might list these answers:

Mom's or Nadine's (of course)

America (Is it like this everywhere? It can't be, can it?)

other industrialized countries (Is rising consumerism what drives this? Where else is gift-giving so woven into the cultural fabric?)

on TV (Are we reacting to commercialism?)

at church (Is it a religious value?)

in magazines (*Real Simple*? *O*? That Martha Stewart magazine?)

Why? This question looks for causes of the "What?" events. This is one of the better questions because it forces you to look beneath the surface of the topic and into the underlying relationships of actors to their motivations and to the effects of their actions. Using the word "because" in your sentence helps you to guess why something might be happening.

Here are some examples:

Some people today give handmade gifts because it makes them feel good about themselves.

Handmade gifts are valued more now because they feel like a throwback to "the good old days."

Americans tend to value handmade gifts over store-bought gifts because they are sick of commercialism and consumerism (not because they actually like anything homemade).

I don't like handmade gifts because I don't have the time to make them (and maybe I wish I did).

How? This question looks at the methods or the manner in which things happen. It's another question that will help you to make connections and explore beneath the surface of a topic. Like "Why?" questions, "How?" forces you to use complete sentences, and these lead you toward an idea you might use in your essay. Use the word "by" in your sentence to make this connection.

Here are a few examples:

> People react against popular culture by making handmade gifts.
>
> Some people (Mom, Nadine) undercut the actual value of healthy gift-giving (fellowship, thoughtfulness) by using handmade gifts to (possibly) validate all the time and money they pour into their hobbies. (Do they feel insecure about how they spend all that time and money?)
>
> Others (like me) reinforce the false valuing of handmade gifts (even thoughtless ones) by acting as if they are truly valuable. (Why am I storing 25 quilts? Why not give them to Goodwill?)

The reporters' questions won't themselves be good questions at issue for an essay because they will mostly be answered by facts instead of opinions. However, you should find something within the "Why?" and "How?" sections that might work as the question at issue for your essay. In the examples above, several side questions came up during this process. These might be dead ends if they aren't debatable or answerable, but they might also lead to a good question for an essay. I wonder, for example, why handmade gifts are considered more thoughtful when it takes so much thought to shop online. And why are handmade gifts thoughtful when the person makes it while sitting in front of a TV, mindlessly knitting a sweater? Is all of this simply nostalgia for times past? These questions might be worth checking out.

BROWSING

Freewriting and the reporters' questions all help you to find an engaging questions from *inside* your brain — or at least they help to jump-start your brain into more active thinking about a seemingly boring topic. Browsing is a technique that looks *outside* your brain for information, ideas, and other forms of inspiration that might lead to a good question.

It's a simple procedure. You visit your library's reference section, search the Internet, search the article databases for magazines, newspapers, and so on, and see what's out there related to your assigned topic. You aren't looking for evidence at this point because you don't know what your question will be. You're looking to see how others divide a topic into subtopics and, more importantly, you're looking for questions that have mattered to other writers.

General reference works, like encyclopedias and subject dictionaries, break topics down into smaller subtopics. This helps you narrow your search by choosing a smaller topic, and it might point out matters of disagreement within that topic. Magazine and newspaper databases give you the titles of articles and essays related to a topic. Take a good look at those titles. Often they focus on a controversy of some sort, and a controversy is just a bunch of answers fighting over who gets to answer a single question. If that question also matters to you, it might make a good question for your essay.

MAKE SURE YOUR QUESTION IS A QUESTION

Once you've identified a question that matters to you and fits your assignment, it's a good idea to make sure the question really is debatable and answerable. If there's only one reasonable answer to the question, you'll end up with a report about that accepted answer rather than an essay about your own opinion. If there's no way for you to gather relevant evidence — either because it doesn't exist or you can't get your hands on it — then your answer will be unverifiable guesswork and of little value to you or your readers.

If you found your potential question by browsing, you probably don't have a lot of checking to do. You wouldn't have found printed articles if the question wasn't debatable and answerable by others. If you found your question with one of the other techniques, however, you should do some checking now to make sure you're heading in a good direction. This is especially true when you freewrite because you're being led by your curiosity, and your curiosity may be ahead of its time.

One way to check out a question is to look for magazine and newspaper articles related to it. This requires some key-word searching, and if you haven't done that before, this will also require a little help from your local reference librarians — or the handouts they created to keep you from bothering them. That's nothing to worry about. If searching reveals that others have written about the topic, there's a good chance that evidence is out there. If you find more than one answer to your question, then you know it's debatable.

If you're writing for a particular class, you can also make sure your question is a good one by talking to your professor. Nobody talks to professors about writing assignments. You can see the sadness in their faces. Here they've spent decades studying and thinking about these topics, and the only questions they get from student writers are about midterms and grading curves. They're *dying* to share what they know, so ask them what they think about your question. They'll be honest with you, and they'll get you started with some good sources of evidence. Depending on how lonely they are, they might even make copies. This could be really positive for both of you.

THE KEY TO SUCCESS: ASK A SMALLER QUESTION

Although it seems to go against common sense and your own experience in writing all those high school reports, one great secret about writing a successful college essay is that you should always ask the smallest question possible. The more you reduce the size of your question, the more effective your essay becomes. It's really that simple. With less evidence to consider, you have more time to study the details of that narrower band of evidence. The work becomes more engaging. Your answer becomes more complex and insightful. Your essay will be more detailed and vivid.

You ask a smaller question by narrowing your focus to a smaller slice of your topic. If, for example, you are assigned the seemingly awful topic of houseplants, you might narrow your focus to one type of houseplant (begonias) or one requirement for raising houseplants (regular attention) or one benefit of having houseplants (companionship). Look for the most interesting subtopic within your current topic and then reduce your question so that it asks about that subtopic.

Accomplish less, in other words. You probably don't get that advice very often, but it's good advice, and not just for writing. I wish I'd never heard the words "you can be anything you want to be." The truth is, you can be anything you want to be *within reason*. It only took me thirty-five years to figure that out.

With regards to writing, though, asking a big question — about the morality of abortion, the impact or existence of global warming, or whether corporations should be entitled to free speech protection — merely starts you on the road to a C essay because that kind of question requires more evidence than you or your essay can handle. In the past, you might have had nice teachers who patted you on the back for that sort of "big-picture thinking," but those teachers were only nice because they had pensions to look forward to and health benefits. Most of your college professors are not so fortunate.

Instead of writing about a big topic, write about a small topic and then make your question even smaller by focusing on a subtopic of that small topic. Instead of asking a big, impressive question about how things *are*, ask a smaller question about whether something is possible or what a single case study suggests about the big topic. That's what I mean by accomplishing less. It requires less evidence, so you can then look more closely and thoughtfully at that smaller collection of evidence.

If you ask whether houseplants make better companions than animals, for example, your question is unusual and potentially engaging but still much too large. It asks about all houseplants and all animals. Think of all the evidence you'd need to figure out a reasonable answer. You couldn't fit it all in an essay. However, if you ask whether plants *might* be better companions than animals, you only need to find out whether it's happened before or that it could logically happen under the right conditions. This is therefore a question that you can answer more clearly, with lots of detailed evidence, in a short essay.

If your paper has to meet a minimum length requirement, you might think that a big question will guarantee a longer paper. It doesn't. The big answer required by a big question forces you to rely on summarized rather than detailed evidence. Summaries can be written quickly, with fewer words. As an added negative, summaries also tend to be less vivid because those summarized points lack the power of detailed evidence to stimulate your readers' imaginations.

Suppose that your topic is math and your purpose in writing is to answer this question: How important is math in daily life? With a big question like this, you'll need massive amounts of explanation and evidence because almost every aspect of daily life has a direct or indirect connection to math. You might offer a few detailed examples — balancing a checkbook, figuring out what kind of mileage your 1986 Honda Civic gets, and so on — but those examples won't adequately defend an answer to the question because they cover only a small part of daily life. To adequately answer this question, you need to cover all or most of the math-related aspects of daily life, and that will require summaries of the broad range of necessary information and examples. You'll end up with paragraphs that look like this:

> Math is also important in household activities. Math may be used to balance the checkbook and make budgets. It might also be used to determine the cost of vacations or weekend trips. It can be used in shopping to compare the relative cost of similar products and help determine the most economical product to purchase. With just about every household activity, math is close at hand.

The summaries in that paragraph cover a lot of evidence quickly, but that doesn't help you get the length you need. So while the old principle of report-writing still works — the broader the topic, the more information you have to work with — covering more information does not mean a longer or more effective essay. It means the opposite.

When you start to reduce the size of your question, the immediate result is that you remove information from consideration. Suppose you reduce "How important is math in daily life?" to "How important is geometry in daily life?" That eliminates all forms of math except for geometry. Reduce your question further to "How important is plane geometry in residential construction?" Now you remove almost all the original topic and can finally get into the details of evidence. You might explore how the Pythagorean theorem, for example, is used by framing carpenters to make sure walls are built square:

> One common use of plane geometry occurs whenever a framing carpenter needs to lay out where to put the walls of a house. It's essen-

tial that the walls are square (that is, with the junction of walls forming true right angles). This makes the work of drywallers and finish carpenters much easier because they will be able to make all their cuts quickly without having to take the time to compensate for walls and corners that aren't square. To make sure the walls are all laid out square, the framer uses the Pythagorean theorem: $A^2 + B^2 = C^2$. If Wall A, for example, is 30 feet long, then A^2 would be 900. If wall B is 40 feet long, then B^2 would be 1600. If Wall A and Wall B are joined at a true right angle, then the distance from the far end of Wall A to the far end of Wall B will be the square root of 900 plus 1600. The sum of 900 plus 1600 is 2500. The square root of 2500 is 50. If Wall A and Wall B are laid out square, the diagonal that connects their far ends would be 50 feet long. If the framer makes sure these lengths are exact, the walls will be square.

If math gives you stomachaches, then this detailed illustration of math for carpenters isn't going to do much for you — except give you a stomachache. Even so, you can still appreciate how this detailed example illustrates the practical use of math more clearly than the previous summaries of huge ideas.

You should try to reduce the size of your question whenever you can. Even in that initial work of phrasing a question, watch out for vague terms that ask for more information than you have time to gather. Replacing broad terms (math, society) with precise terms (algebra, carpenters) makes the question smaller.

As you check to make sure your question is a real question, you will also get a sense of how much information is out there. If you printed it up, would it fit in your backpack? Would it fit in your car? Would it fit in a truck? The larger the vehicle required to carry your evidence, the more reason you have to ask a smaller question, gas prices being what they are.

Once you have your question figured out and begin to gather and consider relevant evidence, you might discover that you have more evidence than you have time for. That's a sure sign that your question needs to get smaller. I can offer two ways to make the question smaller. First, you can focus on a subtopic within your current topic. Because you know your topic better, you also know which subtopics attract more debate. Any of those subtopics will be a good focal point for a smaller question because of that ongoing discussion. If you still have too much to do, you can narrow your focus to a *sub*-subtopic or you can look for a different subtopic that's still interesting but less crowded with debate or evidence.

Your second option is to stick with the bigger question but narrow its focus to a single case study as a way of exploring the larger issue. If you really want to keep the bigger question of whether education significantly impacts the lives of teenage mothers, for example, you could look at one or a few teenage mothers who have — or have not — had access to education. The evidence from those case studies won't be enough to answer your big question, but it will be enough to support an answer about whether something is *possibly* true.

Presenting a possibility might not seem like much of a main idea for an essay, but that's how it works with most arguments, even when the questions are narrow. If there's enough evidence out there to establish a fact, then there's probably no need for an argument. Argument tends to show up where the evidence is weaker, and establishing reasonable possibilities is what argument does best.

It's also no small thing to get readers to consider a new possibility. They might have looked at this issue before and thought they had it figured out. If you can show them that a new answer might be better than an old one, you get your readers thinking again. That in itself is a worthwhile accomplishment.

Chapter Four

CONSIDER THE
EVIDENCE

The second step in the writing process is to gather and consider evidence that's relevant to your question. Before you get started, though, please remember one thing — don't be a knucklehead about it.

When you look for evidence with a mind that's already made up, you tend to accept the facts that support your idea and reject everything else. You become entrenched in the ideas you started with. Where's the fun in that? Instead, make this search for evidence your own personal mission to find the best answer available. That's an essential attitude to take if you're going to write a good college essay and avoid drifting into the lunatic fringe.

In this chapter, you'll look at different sources of evidence to consider and how to make the most of them. You'll also consider their limitations. It's beyond the scope of this modest text to explain the intricacies of academic research, but this will at least get you moving in the right direction.

CONSIDER CREDIBILITY AND OBJECTIVITY

With sources of evidence, you look for two main qualities — credibility and objectivity. Credibility is a measure of how well a writer or publication is qualified to gather and report information about your topic. When it comes to interpreting the meaning of the information, it's even more important that the writer is credible. Objectivity is a measure of the degree to which a source presents specific, real-world information rather than the summary or interpretation of that information. The more a source relies on facts, the more objective that evidence becomes.

With news articles, for example, the writer is a reporter. This is someone who's trained to gather and report information about current events, so that's a plus if you are looking for that kind of information. However, the quality of reporting tends to be reflected by the quality of the newspaper, too. A reporter for the *Bozoville Itemizer-Herald* probably lacks the experience or skills — and thus the credibility — that you will find in a reporter for a major daily newspaper. Similarly, a reporter for a tabloid has to follow the tabloid's nasty habit of making stuff up. Tabloid articles won't be as credible as the generally factual articles of a traditional newspaper.

The newspaper isn't the only place that reports news, of course. You also have websites that report news. Some magazines summarize the news, and some offer expanded coverage and analysis. You have television programs and radio programs and books written after the fact that look deeply into the particulars of what used to be news. The subjects of news stories might release their own information directly to the public in blogs. Others write books telling "their side" of a story. You might have seen news happen firsthand, making you a source. No matter where they come from or what they report, however, these sources of evidence can all be judged by the same two standards: How credible is the source? Is the evidence objective?

And that's just for news. The same two questions should also be asked about publications of historical evidence, scientific data, professional practices, textual studies, political analysis, biography, and so on. When you search for evidence with an Internet search engine, the resulting list of websites makes them all look like equals. They aren't equal, though, and it's up to you to look more closely and judge carefully. It's also up to you to stop relying so heavily on Internet search engines. I don't care how easy it is. Those search engines are owned and operated by people trying to make money from you. Beware!

In the next section, you'll look at sources that are a good starting point — general sources that provide summarized information about a wide range of subjects. Then you'll look at some better sources of evidence to use as you become more involved in your research — sources that provide more detailed evidence for a general audience. The best sources, you will see, are usually those written by and for professional audiences. In each case, the two qualities that make a source good, better, or best are the credibility of the writer and publication and the objectivity of the evidence.

START WITH GENERAL SOURCES

At the shallow end of the evidence pool, general sources introduce you to a topic and its terminology. They help you to find and check out a good question and then narrow your focus to make that question smaller and better. The evidence in general sources is safe and it's shallow, which is perfect when you don't really know what you're doing with your topic. You won't drown in the shallow end without considerable effort.

A general source covers a broad range of topics for either a popular or professional audience. A dictionary is the most common general source of information. A language dictionary covers all the words in a language. A medical or legal dictionary covers all the terms or topics within that somewhat narrower focus. Encyclopedias are also common general sources. General encyclopedias attempt to briefly explain *everything*. Topical encyclopedias — an encyclopedia of religion or zoology, for example — are just as ambitious within their reduced boundaries.

The Internet has opened the door to new types of general sources. Many government agencies put their policies online. City councils and state governments provide transcripts or recordings of their meetings. Online databases have appeared for every topic. Do you need to know when the next Nicolas Cage movie will appear? Any of several online movie databases can tell you. Judging the value of general sources requires the same two questions from the previous section.

First, are the writers and publications credible? With printed general sources, the answer is usually yes. That's because dictionaries and encyclopedias are expensive to create. They require significant funding and a lot of coordination, so if it ever gets done, it's usually done by qualified professionals. Any printed dictionary, for example, is the work of scholars, and the same is true of other published general sources. Many fully electronic sources are also the careful work of trained professionals: Government websites are produced by agency professionals who understand their subject areas very well. Many printed sources also provide electronic versions of the same publication, and these are just as credible.

Some websites, however, use reader input to create their content — book reviews, travel guides, dining reviews — and these are less credible. With a book review site, for example, the author of a review *might* be qualified to judge the quality of a book. However, the reviewer might also be an intern working for the publisher of that book. She might be the still-angry former girlfriend of the author. He might be a precocious thirteen-year-old who finds joy from inserting his dog's name into his reviews. She might be my mother, who never rates anything highly because she doesn't want to encourage self-esteem. Reader-generated sites rarely use trained editors to screen out dumb or biased reviews, so you have to be more careful judging the objectivity of each review.

Some reader-generated sites *are* credible. The difference tends to be editorial oversight and a more professional readership. With many professionally focused websites — for plumbers, computer programmers, graphic designers — the reader input is moderated by trained professionals who weed out lousy input and provide their own detailed and credible commentary. Because of that oversight, the credibility of the site rises.

In the case of the world's most famous online encyclopedia, Wikipedia, there are several levels of editorial review and often fierce debate among competing viewpoints. That editorial review, along with citations of sources and a generally more informed and professional set of contributors, makes this online encyclopedia much more credible than many grumpy old professors are willing to admit. It's still possible for any idiot to corrupt an article with bad information — "The water buffalo makes a great pet." — or something silly — "I miss you, Deedee!" — but that kind of junk is quickly removed.

Textbooks are another general source you should consider. They're written by knowledgeable authors for a general audience. They're good at explaining important terms related to the topic and providing a comprehensive overview. They're also good at presenting the debatable issues. That's just the sort of thing you need when you're getting started.

The second question to ask is how objective is the evidence in general sources. Because the focus of general sources is so broad, the evidence they provide is equally broad and thus shallow. They rely on summaries and key pieces of information rather than detailed evidence. Because the writers are usually credible professionals, you can trust those summaries more than if they came from a journalist or volunteer contributor, but they're still summaries rather than objective evidence. Government websites can be an exception to this rule. Because of the relatively cheap cost of online publishing, government websites will often provide both broad summaries and the objective, real-world details they summarize.

As long as the writers are credible, general sources are still good to use early in the writing process. When you need to test out a possible question, those summaries will quickly show you whether the question is debatable or answerable. If you're interested in whether Seasonal Affective Disorder is really a disease, for example, a medical encyclopedia will let you know that of course it is, and that if your sister or anyone else thinks otherwise, they're wrong and insensitive. General sources can also point you toward other questions that might be better for a college essay.

Another good use of general sources is to help you ask a smaller question. A dictionary helps you translate general terms into more precise ones. You can replace a broad word with just one of its possible definitions. Topical dictionaries are even better for asking smaller questions with more precise terms. Other reference works help you find interesting sub-topics and pockets of debate. These improve your question by giving it narrower boundaries so you can look more closely at that smaller set of evidence. They also show you which topics are most interesting to scholars. That's where you'll find the best evidence to consider.

But don't stop here in the shallow end of the evidence pool. Although you have good reason to trust the summaries of credible sources, that's not the same as getting into the details of evidence and making up your own mind about what those details mean. That's where most of your work should take place.

Use Serious Popular Sources to Explore

In the middle of the evidence pool, popular sources help you to understand some of the complexities of your topic, to refine your question further, and to start uncovering primary texts and scholarship. They get you closer to the better evidence but don't force you to swim through it on your own. You can still touch bottom here, which is reassuring to your fragile nerves. Reading popular sources is like going back to Pollywogs for a swim lesson. You might not be able to swim yet, but at least you have cute high school girls in swimsuits to teach you how it's done.

Popular articles are written by professional writers — the cute swim teachers — for broad audiences of readers who aren't yet ready for the deep end. These publications are there to make money, and they make their money by targeting popular issues and exploring them thoughtfully. However, don't confuse these serious publications with the far more popular and far less serious publications that focus on celebrities and how to make your hair look like celebrity hair. Their role is primarily to make plane flights seem shorter or give you something to do while visiting your dentist. That's fine for what it is, but serious popular sources have a bit more to offer than that.

Newspapers are the most common type of serious popular source. They rely on professional journalists to gather information from credible sources, to confirm the validity of that information, and to present that information objectively. They cover a wide array of events, usually in brief articles. With engaging or controversial events, they might explore the details in more depth, including evidence from scholars, local authorities, and others who have a professional relationship to the topic.

Not all newspapers are credible, of course. Tabloid papers, for example, often ignore real-world evidence and print speculation. They also like to focus on the lurid details that appeal to the fears and lusts of their audience. That's why they're so popular. Small-town papers tend to focus on gentle human-interest stories about their readers so that those same gentle humans will renew their subscriptions. That's nice of the small-town writers, but it's not too useful for argument.

Popular magazines are also written by professional writers, and most magazines use paid editors to double-check the accuracy of that writing. This typically makes the evidence more credible, but the system still allows some junk to get into print. When magazines are more focused (*Architectural Digest*, *Popular Psychology*) or written for a more educated audience (*The Economist*), they often present more thorough and detailed articles about topics than you will find in credible newspapers. Because they are still written for general audiences, though, the language of those articles remains accessible to the average, educated reader.

Trade publications (*American Plumber*, *Insurance Today!*) are written by trained writers, but for a narrower audience of professionals within a specific field. They are sometimes useful for providing information or identifying debatable questions, but the vocational nature of those publications has a way of making them pretty dull work if you're not an actual plumber or insurance agent. They also tend to focus on practical matters within a profession, which further limits their usefulness for you as a writer.

You can put a lot of websites into the popular category, too, because so many are written for general audiences. You need to judge websites as you would printed popular sources — by credibility and objectivity. Government websites typically present summarized evidence and then allow you to dig into the detailed information with little commentary. That's pretty objective. The evidence is gathered and presented by an agency full of people who work with that information, so it's usually credible.

Many other organizations — health societies, political organizations, environmental advocates — also sponsor educational websites that might help you, but here's where things start to get murkier. Each of these groups has a bias, and even if it's a laudable bias, it still gives a slant to the information they publish. The authorship and editorial processes for articles are unclear and vary widely. You might find good stuff, but you can't take it too seriously without corroboration.

For a short essay about a current news story, you are likely to find all you need from serious popular sources. However, for other topics, you eventually have to get into the details of evidence on your own. Professional writers are good at translating complicated evidence into simpler terms for a general audience, but they aren't perfect. To write a good college essay, you need to get as close to the details of your evidence as possible, and you need the most trustworthy sources for that evidence. For that, you need scholarly evidence. You need a good library.

RELY ON SCHOLARLY AND PRIMARY SOURCES

At the deep end of the evidence pool, you find articles and books that are written by scholars, edited by scholars, and, for the most part, read by scholars. For that reason, they are called scholarly sources. You will also find what are called primary texts. These are the texts about which scholars write — novels, plays, movies, poems, musical scores, religious writings, the diaries of pioneers, advertising from the 1940s, and so on. Primary texts are the raw material from which you and the scholars can both draw conclusions. To find the best available answer for your question, you need to get your hands on the most reliable and most detailed evidence available. You need to dive into the deep end of the pool for yourself.

Don't be afraid. Reference librarians will be on duty at all times, walking along the edge of the pool to prevent horseplay and save lives. If you feel yourself starting to cramp up, just wave your arms and they'll toss you a life preserver.

Scholarly writers are the most credible because they are both knowledgeable about their field — the way that a paid professional is — and they're trained in methods of gathering and testing evidence within that field. A fireman is a paid professional who has a lot of practical training and firsthand experience to offer when it comes to fire. A fire scientist, however, is a scholar who has a lot of practical experience with fire but also broader training in the chemistry and behavior of fire — and even more training in methods for studying fire. Moreover, when a fire scientist writes about fire and submits an article or book for publication, other fire scientists scrutinize that writing for the smallest flaws, itching for some reason to reject it. Anything that does get published has to hold up well to that kind of mean-hearted scrutiny.

The training in research methods and the scrutiny of other scholars tend to ensure more objective evidence in scholarly articles and books. The more important factor, however, is that scholarly work focuses more directly on the details of evidence. This allows readers to see for themselves the evidence the scholars have seen and then form their own conclusions or try to replicate the results. These details of evidence are measurable facts rather than the summary or interpretation of facts that show up in popular magazines. They are quotations from and references to primary texts, the quantifiable results of experiments or studies, the exact words of interviewees. They connect the conclusions of the scholars to the real world, and that's what makes this evidence more objective.

For all their virtues, however, scholarly sources have one major drawback. Scholars write these articles for other scholars. They don't mess around trying to explain things to Pollywogs like you. They assume you can already swim, that you're familiar with the topic and the terminology of their discipline. If you're not familiar with the topic or terminology — and there's a good chance you're not, student writer — you will find scholarly sources difficult to figure out. That's not a reason to avoid them, however. That's a reason to be patient as you learn how to swim here in the deep water. It's also a reason to go back to your general sources (especially dictionaries) for help decoding difficult articles and books.

You will find a few scholarly resources online and available to the general public, but you won't find many. It costs a lot of money to produce these works, and even with subsidies from universities or scholarly organizations, a subscription to a journal — that's scholarly talk for "magazine" — is hundreds of dollars a year. Scholarly books are usually expensive, too. Some journals have set up websites of their own, but they're not the free kinds of websites plastered with weight loss ads. Access to articles at these websites often requires individual subscriptions, and it's not uncommon to be charged $10 for access to a single article. Like anyone can afford that on top of rent and cat food.

The best way for student writers to get their hands on scholarly evidence is to do so through a college or university library. In addition to paying for subscriptions to an array of printed scholarly journals, campus libraries also pay thousands of dollars each year for electronic access to even larger collections of journals. Using a campus library, you can search all those scholarly sources for evidence that's relevant to your question. The search systems can be a little daunting at first, but they are all, at heart, regular keyword searches — not unlike how you search with an Internet search engine — so it's not *that* hard to learn, especially with reference librarians just standing around waiting for you to ask for help.

The results of these library searches will be much better than from an Internet search engine, too. When you look at the results, there won't be any defunct websites in the mix. There won't be any fake ads for free laptops. You won't be invited to call Tatiana, an exciting single woman in your area, which I can tell you would be a serious and expensive mistake. Judging from the Jersey accent, I doubt her name is even "Tatiana." When you search for scholarly sources at the library, you get a list of scholarly sources — and that's all. The list might not be as full of mystery and adventure as the list from an Internet search engine, but it will be full of credible authors and objective evidence.

Also in the deep end of the evidence pool are primary sources. These are called "primary" because with these, you become the scholar and deal with the facts of that topic directly. With most scientific topics, you're probably not qualified to work directly with primary sources. You lack the training and money to survey public opinions, split atoms, count the toes on mutant frogs, and so on. For those sorts of topics, you need to rely on "secondary" sources, the writings of scholars who are qualified and have done the primary work for you.

However, particularly in the humanities, your topic will often be a text of some sort, and that's evidence that you *can* work with directly. Whenever your topic is a text — a story, poem, play, essay, and so on — your best evidence will come directly from that text. As a student, you're still learning the methods for exploring and understanding written texts — that's where your classes come in — but you're good enough to get started.

Suppose that you're writing about *Hamlet*, for example, and that your question is whether Gertrude, the Queen, was part of a conspiracy to knock off her first husband. Your best evidence will be the patterns you find in her actual words and actions. In Act 3, for example, the ghost of her first husband appears. Hamlet sees his father, but Gertrude says she doesn't. She's the only person in the play who doesn't see the ghost when the ghost appears. What do you make of that? The evidence you need is as objective as it gets. You have the facts of her behavior right there on the page. That evidence doesn't prove anything outright, but it allows you to be the scholar who decides the significance of these facts. If you can find a logical pattern within that evidence, it becomes a foundation for your answer to that question.

AVOID LOUSY EVIDENCE

Some evidence is better left unused. If you had to guess which two qualities are lacking in that evidence, what would you guess? That's right — they lack credibility and objectivity.

Most lousy evidence shows up in popular publications or on websites that are accessible to the public. You find it in the popular press because reporters and professional writers are sometimes duped by the sources of their evidence. They're sometimes rushed or lazy and fail to double-check evidence. In this way, bad information sometimes finds its way into print. You will find even more bad information on public websites because a basic website is so easy and cheap to set up and operate. Anyone can create an attractive website, and that includes salesmen and bigots and well-intentioned nincompoops.

You don't need to be suspicious of everything, but you should be careful. In the end, you're the one who's responsible for the ideas you let into your brain — and eventually into your essay. What follows are some of the warning signs that will let you know you need to more closely examine a source that may have problems with credibility or objectivity.

HIDDEN AND NOT-SO-HIDDEN AGENDAS

Some writers have broader agendas that might encourage them to interpret or edit evidence to fit those agendas. They might not be full-blown knuckleheads about it, either. The bias might be more subtle than that.

If the author is a politician, for example, he or she almost certainly has policy goals that are important and that, to some extent, define his or her career. This is healthy within the political world. However, if the politician then turns from matters of public policy to other related matters — morality, for example, or nutrition or family dynamics — there's a good chance that the politician's ideas about those topics will be shaped by a topic's relationship to the policy agenda. The evidence might be sound, but you should double-check that.

You should also be wary when the evidence you locate is found inside the website or publication of an organization that has a more obvious agenda. Even when the agenda is one that few disagree with — eradicating poverty, curing cancer, feeding children — it's still an agenda. The organization is thus likely to emphasize evidence that supports their agenda and ignore or downplay other evidence. Even if the evidence that the organization presents is objective, it might be incomplete. An agenda also helps to shape the website editors' views about what the evidence means. Again, it might be sound evidence, but double-check their interpretations.

MISSING CREDENTIALS

You might find writers who sound reasonable enough but have no actual credentials — professional or scholarly. Be careful with them. They might be geniuses who are actually too smart to make it through the public school system. They might be well-meaning amateurs. They might be knuckleheads. If what you read makes sense and is supported by objective evidence, then I say take them seriously. But also double-check their work. See what others have to say about it. Get a broader range of evidence to consider.

A related problem happens when people who have been successful in one profession offer comments about a subject in which they are not qualified. When professionals stray from their area of expertise, the value of their opinions quickly diminishes. It's like the actor in a commercial telling you, "I'm not a doctor, but I play one on TV." So tell us about acting, then, but keep your strange ideas about aspirin to yourself. In the same way, a respected preacher's ideas about politics or a professional basketball player's ideas about religion shouldn't be given any more weight than anyone else's personal observations and opinions. There might be something there, but I wouldn't count on it if I were you.

Missing Evidence

If there's no evidence defending an author's opinion, then there's no reason to take that opinion seriously. You see this all the time in advertising. Some toothpaste is now fresher than ever. Some candidate is just what your state needs. Those opinions don't mean anything because they haven't been explained or defended with actual evidence. The advertisers are simply pushing the ideas into your brain and hoping the ideas will stay there long enough to influence your money or your vote. You know that, right? Of course you do.

You also know that you shouldn't take seriously the same sort of undefended assertion when it's quoted in news stories or posted online or spouted by knuckleheads on knucklehead news programs. My local paper has a regular feature called "The Daily Rant" where each day one knucklehead is allowed to complain about something without having to defend it. You wouldn't use any of these ideas in a serious argument. There's always the possibility that an undefended idea is true, but if the evidence to defend an idea exists, the ranters should have mentioned it. When you see an interesting idea that comes without any defense, don't use it until you've first tested it with relevant evidence.

The most tempting undefended ideas are in interviews. Interviews are usually one raw assertion after another with little time or interest given to supporting evidence. Nonetheless, they're usually interesting because the people interviewed are interesting. The perspectives can be engaging for a lot of reasons. If the interviewee is qualified to speak on a topic, you might still check out those opinions and test them with relevant evidence. The comments might point you in a good direction. But even then, it's the objective evidence you uncover that should help you make up your mind much more than the interview.

UNVERIFIABLE EVIDENCE

Sometimes writers are sneaky, and sometimes they are outright dishonest. You need to be vigilant about such writers. Their bad ideas have a way of hurting people, and when you let their bad ideas into your own thinking or your essay, you become an unwitting accomplice.

One warning sign of dishonesty is unverifiable evidence. This is evidence that the writer presents in support of an idea but without telling you where it came from or, in the case of summaries, without giving you the details that are summarized. It's unverifiable because the author doesn't allow you to verify it. This evidence might look sensible, but if the writer won't tell you where it came from, you can't take a closer look at the particulars or the source to verify that it's dependable.

I recently read this line on a college website: "89% of faculty support this initiative." The initiative was an administrative maneuver to gradually replace actual faculty with standardized "course shells" operated by "instructional specialists." I've never seen 89% of faculty support *anything*, much less a ploy to outsource themselves. When the website failed to offer where this number came from, I became mildly suspicious. It might be that 89% of faculty do indeed support this initiative, but I will need to see the details behind that statistic before I'm willing to accept it.

As in this case, you must be particularly vigilant with statistics. Statistics look like facts because they're made out of numbers, and numbers look objective. People are suckers for numbers. However, statistics are really just summaries of detailed evidence. They are often interpretations of those details. They are thus easily manipulated to become questionable interpretations of those details. When you don't see any way to verify those statistics, you should be on your guard at least 89% of the time.

Personal Experience

Personal experience and observation are other kinds of unverifiable evidence of which you should be wary. Personal experience and observation give you good questions to consider, and they might be good ways to engage your readers' imaginations in an opening, but they rarely explain anything because the scope is so limited. People are generally clueless, too — not you, of course, but everyone else. They frequently misunderstand their own experiences. They remember a lot of things the way they wish things had happened.

When used as a bit of color to *illustrate* an idea, personal experience is fine. Have fun with it. Imagine yourself in that situation. When a writer uses personal experience to *defend* an idea, you should be skeptical. It might indeed be evidence for the idea, but it's almost certainly not sufficient evidence.

TAKE NOTES, TOO

The more time you spend considering evidence, the more you need to keep track of what you find and where it comes from. This is serious work. You need to keep track of the information you find and where you find it so that later, if you decide to use it in your essay, you can use it correctly. To make your evidence verifiable, you have to know where it came from.

The best way to keep track of your evidence is with note cards. Usually, you keep two sets of cards. With one set, you record the sources of evidence you find, using one card for each source. With the other set, you record each piece of evidence — usually a summary but sometimes a quotation — on its own card and identify the source. You might have ten evidence cards from a single source.

I don't just say that note cards are the best system because I'm an old fart. I say that because it's true. And never mind that the last time you saw anyone use note cards was when your grandma copied a snappy tuna casserole recipe out of the newspaper. Your grandma was a wise woman. By putting each bit of evidence on its own note card, you create a level of control over your evidence that cannot be found in any other system — electronic or otherwise.

Is that right, says the smug student writer, who has not used a pencil since fourth grade.

Yes, that's right. It might be true that using note cards to record the evidence is something of a dying art, like building cathedrals or typing. But it's still the best option you have here in the deep end of the evidence pool. But even if you're not willing to use note cards, you still need to keep track of the information you find.

Many student writers print out or photocopy potential sources of evidence and call that note-taking. If that's your method, then every time you print out or photocopy a source, the first thing to do is staple the pages together so that they won't commingle with pages from other sources. That's not taking notes. That's just preventing potential heartache. To actually take your modern version of notes, you need to mark — on those photocopied and laserprinted pages — the actual bits of evidence that are relevant to your question. Do this with a bright highlighter. Don't use Post-it notes. Post-it notes have just enough sticky stuff to stay in place until you turn your back on them. Then they fall off, breaking your heart.

You can also mark your evidence with durable plastic arrows that stick more firmly to the page and jut out beyond the edge of the paper. These are the plastic arrows that lawyers put on contracts and divorce papers in case you're too distraught to figure out where to sign. Those plastic arrows are kind of expensive, but they stay put and will continue to point to the evidence for a long time.

If you're going to rely on photocopies, it's also a good idea to keep a separate list of the evidence you find. If you find a good paragraph in an article, for example, you then add that to your list by noting the author's name, the page number, and a very short summary of the idea or information. This kind of list makes it easier to keep track of what you find and retrieve it later from your stack of photocopies. It's not as good as note cards, but it's as close to note cards as the digital age has come.

Chapter Five

DECIDE ON THE
BEST ANSWER

Gathering and considering evidence can be surprisingly enjoyable, particularly if the only one waiting for you at home is the cat your former girlfriend left behind. As you do your detective work, you learn things you didn't know before. This is especially true when the assigned topic or question isn't something you would have chosen for yourself. The dull exterior of the topic opens to reveal unexpected and sometimes pretty cool complexities you wouldn't have noticed otherwise. You start to make discoveries for yourself, discoveries that you can't help but share with your friends or your family or the cat until they tell you, in so many words, to shut up. This is good work for you and your brain.

At some point, however, you run out of time. That's how it works inside the time-space continuum — too much space and never enough time. Everything is going great, and then you happen to look at the clock and say to yourself, "Gosh. This essay's due in six hours," or words to that effect. When you reach this point in the writing process, evidence-gathering must stop and decision-making must begin. You need a main idea for the essay you're about to draft, and that main idea has to be what you decide is the best available answer to your question.

This really is a decision, too. In the same way that a judge decides a verdict, you need decide an answer to your question. You determine that answer based on the evidence you have now, the evidence that was available to you. That answer might change over time as more evidence becomes available and you become a better judge of evidence, but don't worry about that. It's time to start writing now, so you have to make the best decision you can at the moment and go with it.

In this chapter, you'll look at how to make this decision. It's a two-part process. First, you inventory the evidence you've gathered so you can decide what it tells you. Second, you refine that answer so that it matches your evidence as honestly and precisely as possible. Once you've taken these steps, you'll have the main idea of your essay *and* a good idea about what evidence that essay will require.

LET YOUR EVIDENCE GUIDE THIS DECISION

This decision about the answer to your question has been hanging around your evidence-gathering from the start. You've tinkered with possible answers each time you picked up a new article or book. You've probably found yourself thinking about it while driving or watching TV or when you should be listening more closely to whatever it was your sister called to complain about. One way to process the evidence is to let your brain kick it around informally in this way. However, when it comes time to decide what your answer will be, you should step back for a moment and take inventory of what you've discovered so that you don't overlook anything important. This allows you to more thoughtfully understand the patterns in your evidence.

How should you take inventory? If you're using note cards, you simply unleash their awesome, low-tech power. You lay the note cards out on the dinette table and move them around. I know that doesn't sound like much, but trust me — it's awesome and powerful. Note cards allow you to visually arrange the evidence into its natural patterns. Those patterns might be steps in a process, competing answers, or different subtopics within the topic. It's different with every question and every set of evidence, but note cards are great for allowing you to look for patterns in the evidence you've collected.

It's harder to do this when you don't have note cards, but it's not impossible. You just have to remember that you are taking inventory of *evidence*, not of sources. If your idea of taking notes has been to print out or photocopy entire chapters or articles, you must now pull from these sources a list of the actual bits of evidence that you find relevant to your question. If you were making that list as you gathered evidence, you're looking pretty smart right now. You don't look as smart as you would if you had note cards awesomely spread out on the dinette table, but you certainly look smarter than the student writers who are now staring sadly at a stack of photocopies.

Your inventory should be a list of all the bits of information that you highlighted or circled or pointed to with plastic arrows or flagged with Post-it notes that have fallen off and collected in the bottom of your backpack. You probably have several pieces of evidence from each source, so each piece of evidence should be listed as a separate item in your inventory. Next to that item, note its source. That will save time later on.

Suppose your question is about William Shakespeare's play *Hamlet* and why Hamlet's mother, Gertrude, married her brother-in-law so soon after her first husband's death. This might be a list of the evidence you gathered:

1. Gertrude's marriage protects Prince Hamlet from attack by political rivals (Powers).

2. Gertrude's marriage protects Prince Hamlet from Claudius's insecurity (Blain).

3. Gertrude's words in Act 1, Scene 2, suggest she was having an affair with Claudius prior to King Hamlet's death (Nousen).

4. Act 3, Scene 3: Gertrude admits there's no comparison between Claudius and King Hamlet, suggesting she doesn't admire Claudius.

5. Act 3, Scene 1: Gertrude gets the point from the play within a play, that it's meant to offend Claudius, which suggests she may have been in on the plot.

6. Act 2, Scene 1: Gertrude keeps pushing Claudius on Prince Hamlet as his new father, which seems pretty clueless. She's probably doing this for herself more than for her son.

7. If Gertrude doesn't marry Claudius, Prince Hamlet has no chance of ever being king (Roby).

8. Act 5, Scene 2: Gertrude distances herself from Claudius and focuses

on Prince Hamlet, suggesting that her son is her primary concern.

9. Act 5, Scene 2: When Claudius tells Gertrude to not drink the poisoned wine, she does anyway. She might have done this to protect Prince Hamlet from the poison. She also disobeys Claudius, which suggests disrespect, which is a vote against love.

10. Act 1, Scene 2: Gertrude begs Prince Hamlet to stay at the castle and be close to her, so in her mind, the more important alliance might have been between her and her son.

That's not a bad inventory. You have some relevant primary evidence here from the play. Assuming those names in parentheses refer to the authors of scholarly articles, then you have a lot of relevant secondary evidence, too.

The evidence doesn't all point toward any single answer to the question, but we do see a few patterns starting to emerge. One group of evidence suggests that Gertrude may have had an alliance with Claudius prior to King Hamlet's death (items 3, 5, 6). Another group suggests that Gertrude had a lot of concern for her son's future, which might be a better motive for the marriage than love (items 1, 2, 7, 10). A third group suggests that Gertrude didn't think much of Claudius (items 4, 8, 9), which would suggest that she didn't marry him because she was swept away by his awesomeness.

As you put those groups of evidence together, they suggest a few ways you might answer your question. First, you see that there's as much evidence to suggest that Gertrude *doesn't* respect Claudius as there is evidence that she loves him. That makes love for Claudius look like a questionable motive for marriage. Second, you see that Gertrude seems to favor her son a lot. Third, you see that Gertrude's quick marriage to Claudius benefits her son in the long term. If you put those three patterns together, the answer to the question seems to be that Gertrude married Claudius for her son's sake. It's not a slam dunk, but it is a reasonable answer, and it's the best answer this evidence has to offer. If you're going to listen to your evidence — and you are — it seems to say that this should be the answer you decide to adopt as your main idea.

There are other things to consider besides patterns in your inventory of evidence. You also need to consider the quality of the evidence. Suppose that Powers (1) is a brilliant scholar making a thoughtful case for this point that's based on ample objective evidence. Her article appears in the prestigious *Shakespeare Quarterly*. Her idea should be taken more seriously when you inventory the evidence. Put a little star by that item. Meanwhile, suppose that Nousen (3) is an unknown and not very good actor who wrote a short piece for *High School Drama Teacher*. Her idea might be a good one, but her article shouldn't be given the same weight as the Powers essay because she doesn't have the same high level of credibility. Nousen's not a professional scholar like Powers, so put a question mark next to her evidence on your inventory list.

The primary evidence from the play is the most important, and here again, some pieces are better than others because of their direct connection to the question. When Prince Hamlet confronts Gertrude with the difference between his father and Claudius in Act 3, Scene 3, Gertrude clearly agrees and begs him to stop (4). It's not a big logical step from there to the conclusion that she doesn't think much of Claudius, so that's a solid piece of evidence to consider. Give it a star. However, when Gertrude refers to Claudius as Prince Hamlet's new father in Act 2, Scene 1, her motives are unclear (6). She might be clueless about her son's mourning, but she might also see the political danger of Prince Hamlet setting himself apart from Claudius. Because the connection to your question is thin, that bit of evidence isn't as convincing. Give it a question mark.

After you inventory your evidence and identify the patterns within it, it's a good idea to talk with others about your decision. You might talk to other classmates who are familiar with the topic. You might talk with your professor. You might talk to that one friend of yours who is exceptionally good at maintaining eye contact. You might talk to your cat, if you find that helpful. If you don't want to talk to anyone, then writing about your conclusions is a good way to check your reasoning and make sense of your evidence. Just remember that you're not writing the essay by doing this. You're writing as a way to process the evidence, like a journal entry or a long, self-indulgent email to a former girlfriend about all the ways she let you down — an email that of course you never actually send.

As you take inventory, you might notice that your evidence is limited. There's not enough there for you to be certain of your answer. Please respect that condition of uncertainty. It's called the human condition. You think you're able to figure everything out, and then everything goes sideways. It's a drag, I know. The point, though, is that you have to take things as they are. You shouldn't claim more than the evidence tells you. That's borderline knuckleheadism, and it could land you in a Greek tragedy because jumping boldly to the wrong conclusions is *exactly* what tragic Greek heroes do best. Your goal should always be cautious honesty. Let the evidence guide you to the best answer, even if the best answer sounds pretty wishy-washy at first. Wishy-washy is a lot better than boldly sticking your neck out on what you hope is a sure thing and then looking stupid about it. A person can only take so much of that.

FORMULATE AND REFINE YOUR ANSWER

Once you decide on the best available answer to your question, the next step is to put that answer into words and then refine it as a more precise and accurate idea. To do this, you need to use something that writing professors call "the thesis statement."

You might remember the thesis statement from your days of writing five-paragraph trainer-essays. Back in those dark times, the thesis statement was the last sentence of the first paragraph, the sentence that stated that your essay would have three main points to make. We're not talking about that old kind of a thesis statement. The old thesis statement was merely a summary of the essay's contents — child's play.

The college-essay kind of thesis statement is a definition of your essay's main idea — the thesis, the answer to your question. To define that idea precisely, you need a thesis statement that will be far too cumbersome to actually stick into your essay. This kind of thesis statement is a writer's tool. Your readers will never see it. It will work behind the scenes to help you capture and improve your main idea while your thoughts are still fluid. It will give you a clearer purpose before you start to write. This will lead to more successful papers, better grades, higher paying jobs, and ultimately greater attractiveness to the opposite sex. In spite of these obvious rewards for using a writerly thesis statement, many student writers look at the thesis statement not as a useful tool but as a complete waste of time. Wouldn't it be easier, they think, to just write the paper once they have a general direction and all the evidence is still fresh?

Foolish student writers! It only *seems* like a complete waste of time because the quality of your thinking has never mattered before. It matters now. The quality of a college essay depends on the quality of your thinking, not the flow of molten evidence in the same general direction. The thesis statement captures your thinking in advance, and by improving that sentence, you can fix the obvious weaknesses in your thinking before they turn into a dumb essay. This makes the thesis statement one of most valuable tools you have as a writer, and its use is easy enough to learn.

Starting is often the hardest step in using the thesis statement to formulate and refine an idea. It's hard to write a single sentence that clearly states your main idea. It's much easier to write a paragraph or two. It's even easier to leave a vague notion floating around in your brain waves. Consequently, there is a tendency among student writers to work on main ideas "mentally," often over beer with friends. However, one of the great writing secrets is that any starting point is a good starting point. Once you've written a sentence — even a lousy one — you can tinker with it to make it better, and tinkering is easier than starting.

Take this lousy starting point, for example:

Gertrude and her love for Hamlet.

This is a start, but it's still only a topic because it's a sentence fragment, a compound noun phrase. Your answer to the question needs to be a complete thought, so it needs to be a complete sentence, too.

Try again:

Wouldn't a mother love her son more than her brother-in-law?

Okay. That *is* a sentence, and it might not be a bad opening line for your essay, but it's a question. What you need is an answer — an assertion — and for that you need a statement rather than a question. Even if the question, like this one, is rhetorical because it points toward one answer, you need to state the implied answer directly so that you can refine it.

Try again:

I think Gertrude loved Hamlet more.

That's a complete sentence. It's a statement rather than a question. The statement also captures a discovery of yours, which is good. But look at the subject of the sentence — "I." "I" implies that this is an idea about you, that you are answering a question about what you think. What you think is not a real question because there's only one answer to it. No one can argue that you *don't* think this because only you have access to your brain.

So now you need to rephrase this idea so that the idea is an idea about your actual topic — Gertrude — instead of you:

Gertrude loved Hamlet more.

That's better. Now you are out of the picture, and the idea is an opinion about Gertrude. But what was the question? If you're using your inventory list above, the question wasn't about whom Gertrude loved more. The question was why she remarried so soon after her first husband's death. Your thesis statement should be a direct answer to that question, so you can use some of the terminology of the question to help state the answer more clearly.

Try this:

Gertrude remarried so soon after her first husband's death because she loved Hamlet more.

She loved Hamlet more than whom?
Be more precise:

Gertrude remarried so soon after her first husband's death because she loved Hamlet more than Claudius.

Now you have most of the main ingredients from the list of evidence, and you have an opinion about what they mean. But is that really the reason Gertrude remarried Claudius, because she loved her son more than her brother-in-law? That's not quite what the evidence tells you.

This is closer:

> Gertrude remarried so soon after her first husband's death because she wanted to protect Hamlet.

That's much better. You have captured the main opinion of your essay, and you've focused on the topic. Compare that to your starting thesis statement, and you can see the improvement for yourself. There was a time in your life, in fact, when a thesis statement like this inside a trainer-essay would have brought tears to your English teacher's eyes. They grow up so fast, your English teacher would have thought. That time has come and gone. The writerly thesis statement you need now must be more precise and more complete because it's helping you figure out your answer to the question in all its complexity. This writerly thesis statement is for you the writer, not them the readers.

One thing missing from the current thesis statement is an explanation of how remarriage might protect her son. I'll save that for the essay, you might be thinking, and yes, you will certainly include that evidence in your essay. But you should put that part of your thinking in the thesis statement, too, because it's a central component of your answer. To explain how something works, start with the word "by" and then finish that phrase.

Here's how that looks with this idea:

> Gertrude remarried so soon after her first husband's death because she wanted to protect Hamlet by making him a stepson and heir to the new king rather than a potential rival.

That wasn't so hard, was it? And now you have a clearer idea about what to put in your essay. That clarity makes it a better thesis statement. But go back to your list of evidence for a minute. Does that evidence really support this idea?

The reason I ask is that this sentence asserts a fact about Gertrude. It's saying that this *is* the reason she remarried so soon after the death of her first husband. If you started with a good question, then it's a debatable question, right? Right.

The answers to debatable questions are never facts. Your evidence inventory might provide an idea that is *probably* true or *possibly* true, but unless you discovered the secret evidence that has been missing for 400 years and will now end the debate forever, your answer won't be a fact. You have to flee from the temptation to boldly persuade where no one has persuaded before. You must instead present only as much of an answer as the evidence will defend. Try to do that with this idea:

> Gertrude may have remarried so soon after her first husband's death because she wanted to protect Hamlet by making him a stepson and heir to the new king rather than a potential rival.

That's good, but look at your reason. Is it a fact that she wanted to protect Hamlet? As you might be able to tell from the rhetorical nature of this question, it's not.

Try again:

> Gertrude may have remarried so soon after her first husband's death because she may be trying to protect Hamlet by making him a stepson and heir to the new king rather than a potential rival.

That's better. Your evidence isn't overly convincing — and that's going to be the case with most good questions. Someone else might put a different spin on the same primary evidence to reach a different conclusion. The secondary scholarly sources appear to be speculative. With evidence like this, the honest thing to do is to present a possible answer to the question and then use the evidence to prove that it's a reasonable possibility. That's what you've done here. Good for you.

You might feel bad about offering your readers a possible idea rather than a strong and authoritative main idea. You might feel like a wimp. If that's the case, you need to get over that. The bold presenters of big ideas are almost all knuckleheads trying to sell you their lousy ideas with a big show of confidence instead of an honest presentation of evidence. This works great with politics and sales and professional wrestling — but not with the college essay.

With the college essay, you impress your audience with honest use of evidence and your own creative thinking. You use your intelligence and imagination to dig into your evidence and find the most insightful idea that the evidence has to offer. But whether or not you find an insightful idea, you never overstate your evidence for the sake of effect. Be humble about the limitations of your evidence and be honest with your readers. It's better to establish a credible possibility than to boldly present a sure answer that falls apart under closer examination.

You might suppose from this brief sermon that you're done working on the Gertrude thesis statement. You're *almost* done. The missing piece is what to do with the evidence that suggests Gertrude might have also been in love with Claudius and possibly aware of the murder of her first husband. That evidence was hinted at when you started this thesis statement process and asserted that Gertrude loved Hamlet more than Claudius. Here's how you can work that alternate answer into your thesis statement:

> Although some propose that Gertrude may have remarried so soon after her first husband's death because she was involved with or in love with Claudius prior to the murder of the king, her actions suggest it's more likely that she wed Claudius quickly in order to protect Hamlet by making him a stepson and heir to the new king rather than a potential rival.

Now you can stop. Your thesis statement has come a long way in a short time, and you're ready now to start planning how to present your argument, using this thesis statement as your guide. But please, please, *please* remember that this sentence is just for you, the writer. If your readers want to see this idea, they'll have to read the essay that explains the same idea and defends it with all that evidence.

Working so intently on one single sentence might feel difficult at first, but with a little practice you'll find that it's not really so hard if you start with a simple idea — even a lousy one. From there, you can clean it up and expand it into a complex idea. You just have to look at your note cards, if you're a wise student writer, or your inventory list of evidence and continue to check your emerging thesis statement against that evidence until the statement of your idea is precise and complete and, above all, honest.

Many student writers blow off this important work with the thesis statement. They launch into their essays directly from a pile of unprocessed evidence as if everything I've told them is a load of manure. Thanks, they imply with their inaction, for nothing.

Foolish student writers! I understand that inspiration sometimes bails you out in spite of poor planning. Creative phrasing might decorate sloppy thinking just enough to make it appear thoughtful. A professor might read a stack of papers while watching a zombie movie, half-drunk, miserable for company, and in this way miss the fact that you haven't said anything worth saying. Line up enough accidents of fate and you can get by without tinkering with a thesis statement.

However, you will eventually come to a place where you need to make sure your idea is clear and worthwhile before you try to present it in written form. It might not be a college essay, either. It might be a letter of resignation, a business plan, a scholarship application — something that needs to be taken seriously. When that day comes, remember this chapter. The thesis statement will still be a useful tool for you, and this chapter will still be here, too, reminding you about how to use it — as long as you don't sell the book back to the bookstore at the end of the term.

FIND INSIGHTFUL ANSWERS

Your decision about the best available answer should be honest and based on what the evidence tells you. Another quality is insight. A good answer to a question will be one that helps readers to look into this topic and see something they haven't seen before.

Finding an insightful idea requires you to apply your intelligence to the evidence at hand and search it closely for patterns that may not be easy to spot at first glance. You'll recall freewriting and the reporters' questions from two chapters ago. Those tools work to explore evidence, too. Both will help you explore and think about the evidence. They get deeper into the details of the evidence, and that's where you start to discover new patterns and connections. The deeper you go into the details, the less likely it becomes that others have spent time there. That means answers you discover will likely be new for you and for many or all of your readers. Using those techniques may not yield results every time, but they can help you find something new, and that newness is often insightful.

You can also use the thesis statement to make your idea more precise and thorough. That precision transforms a general answer — one that others might already have thought about — into a more complex and sophisticated idea. Even if readers have had the same basic idea, they won't have thought about it in exactly these terms, and that will offer them insight.

But again, student writers, remember that the thesis statement is only a planning device. You're not crafting an elegant line for your first paragraph. You're crafting a grammatical monstrosity for your eyes only — a long, complicated sentence that captures all the pieces of your complex idea. The uglier that writerly thesis statement gets, the closer you are to having an insightful answer. But while that sentence guides you as you draft your essay, it shouldn't ever appear in the essay itself.

Whether you spend more time with your evidence or your thesis statement, your first step toward an insightful main idea is deciding not to settle for an obvious answer. You have to be tougher on your ideas than you've been in the past. You can't treat the first answer that comes along like it's your own little baby. You can't snuggle with it and love it just the way it is. That's a good strategy for raising little babies, but it won't help you make an insightful decision about how to answer your question. A little baby will get smarter on its own, but an obvious idea stays obvious until you do something about it. The harder you study your evidence and work on your thesis statement, the more you'll be able to push past the easy answers and find something better to share.

Here's one last tip for the adventurous. You can drop an obvious answer altogether and go with an alternative answer that's less convincing but more interesting. Just be honest about what you're doing. Tell your readers that your answer is an unlikely possibility, and even that the obvious answer is a better answer, and then have your fun. That advice seems to contradict parts of this chapter and book, but that's life for you. Such paradox! If *you* find your idea engaging, there's a good chance it's an insightful idea, an idea that will engage others. And if it's not all that insightful, then at least you've had some fun.

Part Three

PRESENTING
YOUR ARGUMENT

Once you decide on the best available answer to your question, it's time to turn that answer into an essay. You've probably been waiting for the moment when you can finally let the words flow onto paper. You're almost there. The next three chapters will show you how it's done.

First, you'll plan what goes into that flow of words and how it will be organized. After that, you can start flowing. Enjoy — but only enjoy the body of the essay at first. After you know what the body looks like, you can add an effective opening, a satisfying closing, and plenty of fairly obvious road signs so you don't lose any readers along the way.

Chapter Six

PLAN THE BODY
OF YOUR ESSAY

For the moment, we'll ignore the opening and closing of your essay. Although many writers enjoy spending desperate hours staring at a blank computer screen, waiting for a perfect first line to appear from somewhere in the universe, it's actually a lot easier to write the opening after you've written the body of the essay. By then, you know what to introduce. You also know what evidence you need to summarize in the closing. So for now the opening and closing can wait.

If you enjoy staring at a blank computer screen, you still can, of course. It's peaceful. I get that. However, once you've decided the best answer to your question, the first step in presenting that answer to others is to make a plan.

In this chapter, you'll look at how to make a plan. You'll start out with a brief theory of paragraphs — which you won't skip because you almost certainly need to relearn this — and then you'll see the options you have for arranging all the paragraphs required by your idea.

A BRIEF THEORY OF PARAGRAPHS

Most student writers create a new paragraph whenever they feel like it, and their feelings are guided not by ideas but by aesthetics. They look at the page and see they have accumulated four or five lines of text. This worries them. They don't want the paper to look boring, so they say good-bye to the current paragraph and hello to a new one.

Foolish student writers!

A paragraph, like the essay itself, has a job to do. One part of that job is to make the page look more inviting. By breaking a full page of text into a few smaller sections, the paragraphs tell your readers, Come on, timid reader, it won't be that bad. In this regard, starting a new paragraph whenever you feel like it is not the worst thing in the world. It does make a page look less intimidating, so it fulfills one part of the paragraph's purpose.

However, and more importantly, paragraphs show readers how a long piece of writing is actually a series of smaller units. In your essay, you might explain your main idea with several examples and defend it with several reasons. You can use paragraphs to separate those shorter units from each other so that readers can consider them one at a time. Each example and each reason becomes its own paragraph. Paragraphs do the same work in stories. They divide a large action into smaller steps. With dialogue, they divide the conversation by speaker. In reports, paragraphs divide a large set of information into smaller subsets.

To make good use of paragraphs, then, you must rely on your brain more than your eyes. You need to understand your main idea. You then need to determine which sets of information or examples are needed to explain your main idea and what evidence is needed to show readers that it's a good idea. After you decide what to include in your essay, you can then decide how to use paragraphs to present those parts as smaller units of the whole.

To help make these decisions and share them with your readers, you have a tool called the topic sentence. The topic sentence summarizes — for you and your readers — the job that a paragraph will perform within a longer piece of writing. The rest of the sentences in the paragraph then show readers what you mean. Those other sentences are called supporting sentences. Here's an example of how a topic sentence (in bold) states what the paragraph will explain and how the supporting sentences use details to show readers what you mean by your topic sentence:

> **However, and more importantly, paragraphs show readers how a long piece of writing is actually a series of smaller units.** In your essay, you might explain your main idea with several examples and defend it with several reasons. You can use paragraphs to separate those shorter units from each other so that readers can consider them one at a time. Each example and each reason becomes its own paragraph. Paragraphs do the same work in stories. They divide a large action into smaller steps. With dialogue, they divide the conversation by speaker. In reports, paragraphs divide a large set of information into smaller subsets.

In this case, the "however, and more importantly" tells

readers that one job this paragraph has been given is to respond to the paragraph or paragraphs that precede it. That's a transitional phrase to let readers know that a somewhat different and more important idea is about to be unveiled in comparison to the idea they just read. The rest of the topic sentence then summarizes that somewhat different and more important idea. The supporting sentences help to explain the idea with evidence of how it works with essays, stories, dialogue, and reports.

You don't have to use a topic sentence and supporting sentences in every paragraph you write. If readers can figure out what your paragraph is doing without a topic sentence, you can let them. It'll make them feel good about themselves. There are also times when, to draw attention to a particularly important point, you might use a single sentence as an entire paragraph:

Foolish student writers!

You can't get away with that very often. Even a handful of one- or two-sentence paragraphs in a row make an essay strangely difficult to follow. Writing professors call this "choppiness," and rightly so. They chop the essay into chaotic fragments rather than a neatly divided whole. You can draw attention to an important idea with a short paragraph, but only do that every now and then.

Whether your paragraphs are long or short, with topic sentences or without, remember that their main job is to present one part of your main idea and their secondary job is to make the page less intimidating. If you create your paragraphs randomly or by sight, they might only be doing that secondary job. They might then start to wander from your main idea and look for something else to do. You can avoid this by giving each of your paragraphs the meaningful work it craves. Now that you have a general understanding of paragraphs, the rest of this chapter will show you how to use them in the essay.

Use a Topic Sentence Outline

A topic sentence outline helps you plan the body of your essay by listing the topic sentences for your essay's future paragraphs. You create a rough draft of a topic sentence outline when you inventory your evidence before deciding on the answer to your question. When you start planning how to present that answer in an essay, however, you need to reshape your list a bit. What pieces of evidence do you need to include? How much emphasis should each be given? What evidence *doesn't* stick to your main idea? This kind of outline helps you to think things through before you start to draft your essay.

To build a good outline, you have to think about both parts of the paragraph's job — to show how the main idea is divided into smaller units and to make the essay look more inviting. Start by planning to use one paragraph for each supporting idea or group of information or example. After that, consider the length of your paragraphs. If they will be too long to be inviting, look for ways to divide them into subunits. If you have a lot of short paragraphs that make the essay choppy, look for ways to combine some of them into a longer paragraph.

PLANNING THE ROUGH DRAFT WITH A TOPIC SENTENCE OUTLINE

Let's consider how this might play out with an essay of your own. Suppose your main idea is that February is a terrible month for romance. To explain and defend this idea, you have gathered seventeen supporting pieces of evidence:

1. Flowers are all dead.

2. Birds are gone except for the filthy pigeons that eat garbage all winter.

3. Trees are bare and bleak and depressing.

4. Transportation is an unpleasant challenge for dates.

5. Winter coats are not sexy.

6. Snow pants are not sexy.

7. Rubber boots are not sexy.

8. Runny noses are not sexy.

9. Long underwear is not sexy (usually).

10. There aren't any new romantic comedies in the theater.

11. It's dark by the middle of the afternoon.

12. Seeing people kiss makes me think of germs.

13. The rainy weather makes me want to cry because raindrops are like tears.

14. I cry all the time.

15. My apartment is too cold to have anyone over.

16. My mother can't figure out how to use a thermostat and calls me constantly to come over and set hers the way she likes it.

17. Who would I call anyway?

That's a lot of evidence for this idea, and it adds up to a convincing argument. February truly *is* an awful month. You're also a lot more depressed than you realized. However, some of this evidence is more important than other evidence. The impact of winter coats on romance, for example, is not as compelling as the impact of crying all the time. If you give each point its own paragraph, and if each paragraph is about the same length, you'll suggest to your readers that those points are equally important. That gives the readers the wrong impression about what matters most.

A more likely problem, however, is that the coat paragraph will be pretty short because it's a bit superficial, while the crying paragraph will be pretty long because there's so much complexity to consider. If you have too many of those short paragraphs, the essay becomes choppy. If the long paragraphs get too long, then the essay becomes less inviting. To fix this problem, you combine the shorter, less important points by turning them into supporting sentences for a bigger idea and its paragraph. With an important point whose details would generate an uninvitingly long paragraph, you divide those details into subpoints and give each subpoint its own well-developed paragraph.

Here's what your list of supporting points might look like after some sensible restructuring. Each numbered point now has its own paragraph in the body of your essay. Any lettered points are now supporting sentences within a paragraph:

1. Nature is depressing:

    a. Flowers are all dead.

    b. Birds are gone except for the filthy pigeons that eat garbage.

    c.   Trees are bare and bleak and depressing.

2.   It's hard to go on dates:

    a.   Transportation is difficult.

    b.   No new romantic comedies in the theater.

    c.   My mother can't figure out how to use a thermostat and calls me constantly to come over and set hers the way she likes it.

    d.   Who would I call anyway?

3.   Winter clothing is not sexy:

    a.   Winter coats make you look fat.

    b.   Snow pants make you look fat.

    c.   Rubber boots make your feet look stupid.

    d.   Long underwear looks stupid except in the right lighting and frame of mind.

4.   Health concerns impede intimacy:

    a.   Runny noses are disgusting.

    b.   Seeing people kiss makes me think of germs.

5.   The weather is discouraging:

    a.   It's dark by the middle of the afternoon.

    b.   Rain makes me want to cry because it's so tearlike.

    c.   My apartment is too cold to have anyone over.

6.   I cry in response to the bad weather.

7.   I cry in response to the lack of sunlight.

8.   I cry in response to sad, February-related news stories.

With this restructuring of paragraphs, the planned essay does a better job of focusing on the more important evidence and combining the lesser points so that each of the paragraphs is about as important as the others. It keeps any one paragraph from being too short because of a lack of supporting evidence. It also divides the crying paragraph into three related points so that each can be a well-developed paragraph instead of a single, uninvitingly long one.

Another benefit of the topic sentence outline is that it helps you decide whether a paragraph belongs in your essay at all. This is harder work than you might expect. People are not one-idea-at-a-time creatures, and the more evidence you look at, the more you have to say. It's shockingly easy to get sidetracked here and include stories and examples and information that have nothing to do with your main idea.

In this revised outline, for example, you can see more clearly that while all of this evidence defends the idea that February is a *depressing* month, it's not as clearly connected to the narrower idea that February is a bad month for romance. Is nature, for example, really a necessary part of romance? Do birds have to chirp before you can go to the movies? You might think about cutting that. And bad weather, with the right company, can be great. Haven't you ever heard of snuggling? That's a cheap *and* romantic date. So rethink that paragraph.

And while you're rethinking this evidence, rethink that question about whom you would call. A question isn't a point of evidence. If you want to restate that as a point of evidence, you need to use the answer to that question, which is that you have no one to call. That's not February's fault, so that shouldn't be part of this essay. And the same goes for your mother and her thermostat. She may be annoying, but she's not the reason you're sitting home alone. When you're gathering evidence, it's sometimes hard to separate good evidence from bad or irrelevant evidence, but the topic sentence outline makes it easier to see these distinctions so you can plan a better body.

You don't have to worry about sticking to one main idea when you're just talking over the phone with an old friend. In that context, you can throw together as many ideas and digressions as you like. Nobody cares. But with the college essay, you're only allowed one main idea. You have to make sure that every paragraph in the body — along with all of those supporting sentences— helps you to present that idea to your readers. If a paragraph or sentence strays from your main idea, then out it goes.

REVISING THE ROUGH DRAFT WITH A TOPIC SENTENCE OUTLINE

Even though I require students to hand in a topic sentence outline with their rough drafts, I'm not an idiot. I realize that most students create the topic sentence outline *after* they write the rough draft. Rather than planning the points to include in their rough drafts, they look at the paragraphs they just drafted and pull out the topic sentences. It's hard to stick to one main idea this way. Once the creative process of drafting begins, your mind has a way of going where it wants to, like a big dog pulling you by its leash down a sidewalk or into traffic. Without an outline, it's easy to stray from your main idea.

Even though the topic sentence outline doesn't help these headstrong student writers *plan* their rough drafts, creating a topic sentence outline afterward is still valuable work. If no topic sentence exists in a paragraph, your after-the-fact topic sentence outline points out this deficiency. If that paragraph is well made and actually presents one smaller part of the main idea, you can fix the paragraph by creating a topic sentence. If the paragraph lacks purpose, you can take a quiet moment to rethink the paragraph as a whole. It might be reshaped to present one small part of the main idea — and then given its own topic sentence — or it might be combined elsewhere, or it might be cut from the essay entirely.

Once the paragraphs are confirmed to be functional paragraphs, an after-the-fact outline then identifies which paragraphs stick to the main idea and which do not. It shows you if you are spending too much time on the opening and not enough on the body. It helps you combine small points into larger ones or divide a large point into smaller subpoints so that the paragraphs are neither choppy nor uninviting. We haven't talked about organization yet, but the after-the-fact outline also helps you to organize the paragraphs and correct any paragraphs that stray from your chosen pattern of organization. More about that in a few minutes.

An after-the-draft topic sentence outline is thus a good way to revise your rough draft while it's still pliable. It does take more time to draft, outline, repair, and revise, but it works. So if you find yourself stuck while creating a before-the-draft outline, it won't be the worst idea in the world to go ahead and draft the body of the essay first and then come back and revise it with a topic sentence outline.

ORGANIZE YOUR PARAGRAPHS

When readers understand how the pieces of an essay or story fit together, they have an odd sensation that they can only describe as "flow," as in, "This essay really flows!"

Flows? I ask them. Yes, they tell me. It flows. It really *flows.* That's all I can get out of them, too. The essay has become to them a small stream of thought. What I believe they mean by "flow" is that the essay is organized. It makes sense to them as an orderly series of related ideas.

Organization is not a matter of putting "firstly," "secondly," and "thirdly" at the beginning of paragraphs. Instead, it's the careful arrangement of paragraphs to form a pattern that the readers can then use to organize that evidence in their minds. Some patterns are built into the topics already, and some you can impose on the evidence at hand. Either way, the purpose is the same. Organization shows readers how the pieces of your main idea fit together to form a larger idea — your main idea.

To organize the paragraphs of your essay, you have many options to choose from. Internal patterns are a natural part of the evidence itself, like the chronological pattern within which historical events take place. Logical patterns, such as putting examples in order of importance, emphasize your interpretation of the evidence. And when nothing else works, you can always build a pattern of your own and stick your evidence inside it.

INTERNAL PATTERNS EMPHASIZE HOW THE EVIDENCE IS STRUCTURED

The most effective organization tends to be internal patterns that are already built into a topic or idea or detailed evidence. They keep the evidence organized, but they also reveal the natural structure of the evidence itself. A historical event, for example, is a series of actions and reactions that occur in chronological order. If the topic of your essay is a historical event, you can use the same timeline to organize your own ideas *and* show readers how those smaller moments that make up the event are naturally structured.

Chronological patterns are based on the order in which specific events happened, moving forward or backward. This pattern can be used to present case studies, hypothetical situations, historical events, and predicted future events. **Cause and effect** is a type of chronological pattern that presents either the causes or the consequences of something that happened. You might look at the various causes of an actual or hypothetical event, or at the actual or hypothetical effects of some event, or at both causes and effects. The **problem/solution** pattern is usually chronological, too, because your problem developed in the past, it exists in the present, and you want things to change in the future, first with the solution you propose and then with the effects of that solution.

Spatial patterns arrange the details of your evidence according to the physical location from which the details are taken. These patterns are commonly used with descriptive writing, which tends to describe physical objects and places, but the pattern itself is useful in other situations and in combination with other patterns. You might write about a national crisis, for example, by moving from west to east or south to north with your evidence. **Visual patterns** are spatial patterns that imitate how a camera lens works, moving from a wide-angle view of a situation to a close-up view or vice versa. If you write about how the price of gas affects the economy, for example, you might start with a wide perspective (the nation), narrow to a smaller perspective (the Northeast), and then to an even narrower perspective (a small town in Vermont) before broadening back out (the nation).

Textual patterns are good for essays that ask a question about a particular text, such as a novel, song, film, philosophical essay, and so on. The structure of the text itself serves as an effective pattern for the response. Using this pattern, your essay might follow the order of presentation (Chapter 1, then Chapter 2, then Chapter 3), or it might follow the structure of the thinking (main idea, then main reasons, then supporting evidence), or it might follow one aspect of a text (the use of a particular word in a poem) as it appears. The key is that you're building an essay that's shaped in some way like the text itself.

Internal patterns are effective because they keep readers focused on the structure of the topic as well as the structure of your thoughts. They remind readers how your topics are (or were) arranged in the real world. These are just a few of your options, but it's enough to get you started.

Logical Patterns Emphasize What the Evidence Means

Another option is to organize your evidence with logical patterns that emphasize your interpretation of that evidence. These work well when there isn't a clear internal pattern to unite the body of the essay. They also work when there is a clear internal pattern that works against your main idea.

Suppose, for example, that your question is about the best way to prevent body odor. After considering the evidence, you find there are two effective options — regular bathing and powerful chemicals — and that using powerful chemicals seems to be the better option. To defend your answer, you decide to use an internal problem/solution pattern. You look first at the problem, then at the bathing regularly solution, which came first historically, and then at the powerful chemicals. This gives your entire essay a chronological pattern of organization, and that's fine. However, you can also impose a logical pattern here and put the more effective solution first, regardless of where it fits chronologically, followed by the less effective solution. That's works, too, and with a problem/solution essay, it might make more sense.

This organizational choice is no big deal with just two solutions, but suppose you want to compare five solutions for your body-odor problem. Chronological order might then put your best answer somewhere in the middle of the essay. That's a bad place for your favorite solution because the first and last positions tend to be more memorable for readers. In this case, arranging the solutions from most to least effective instead of chronologically makes a big difference. You can emphasize your best answer by moving it to the front of the line. You can then show why the other solutions, one after the other, do not smell as sweet.

Least-to-most and **most-to-least** patterns are useful whenever you want to present reasons or evidence according to how well they exhibit a particular quality. Any quality will do — effectiveness, cost, size, popularity, morality, importance. Order of importance is popular among student writers, but any quality will do. You then arrange your reasons or examples or sets of evidence in ascending or descending order.

Comparison is a pattern to use when your question is about two or more similar items — objects, ideas, people, events, words — and your solution for answering that question is a side-by-side examination. A fairly common type of comparison essay is one that proposes the best solution to a problem. A medical essay, for example, might compare two treatments for the same condition and draw a conclusion about which is the more effective treatment. A literary essay might compare two characters in a novel and draw a conclusion about who made the better decision.

In setting up the general framework for the comparison, you have two main comparison patterns to choose from, an **alternating pattern** or a **block pattern**. The alternating pattern looks at one aspect of all the compared items (cost, for example), and then at another aspect of all of the compared items (effectiveness, for example), and so on. The block pattern looks at all of the aspects (cost, effectiveness, etc.) of one item (treatment 1), and then at all of the aspects of the next item (treatment 2).

With both of these general comparison patterns, it's a good idea to also arrange your points of comparison according to another pattern — chronological, for example, or most-to-least. That helps readers keep track of them. It's an even better idea to present the details of the comparison in a parallel format. If you look at the cost of deodorants 1, 2, and 3 in that order, then look at the effectiveness of the deodorants in the same order. This helps the readers make a clearer comparison because the details are laid out symmetrically.

Artificial Patterns Work When Nothing Else Does

And then there are times when neither internal nor logical patterns make sense for your evidence or argument. Leaving the evidence disorganized is one option, but it's a bad option. It's better to impose some kind of order than to make your readers put the paragraphs together on their own.

Listing is one of these artificial patterns. It's better than nothing, but not by a lot. In fact, it really only makes sense when you have many smaller points to make and can't figure out any internal or logical order for organizing these details. Perhaps you have seven pieces of evidence to support a proposal, or nine examples of your main idea in action. When that happens, putting your evidence into a numbered or bulleted list makes the evidence *look* organized even thought it's not. If you're going to go into management, a bulleted list is the only pattern of organization you will ever need for your memos and email, but don't rely on that with the college essay.

A second option is the **fake internal** pattern. With this strategy, you create an internal-style pattern (time order, spatial, etc.) that isn't really a part of your evidence and then use that fake pattern as a general framework for the essay. What you're doing is taking something tangible — one typical day, traveling from east to west, a case study — and using that pattern to organize your information. It helps when there's some kind of connection between your information and the pattern you're using, but it's not essential. The fake internal pattern is better than a random list because it gives the body of the essay an actual structure. It also requires some creativity on your part, so it's often satisfying to write. You'll see how that works in the case study that follows.

ORGANIZATION IN REAL LIFE

You might recall the topic sentence outline that supported your opinion that February is a terrible month for romance. That outline doesn't offer an internal pattern of evidence by which you can make this essay flow — really flow — into the minds of your readers. It remains a collection of more or less supporting points, but those points are randomly arranged.

You might improve that outline by imposing a logical pattern on these points. You might arrange them in a least-to-most pattern. You can use the quality "harmful to romance" and move from least harmful to most harmful. Using that pattern, winter clothing might be a good place to start. That pattern might be okay, but with so many points to make, the power of moving from bad to worse to worst is diminished by the number of supporting pieces of evidence that you are ranking.

So what about artificial patterns, then? You could list them. That wouldn't be bad. Because you have so many complaints, a list does emphasize that high number. It underscores how many things are wrong with this month. A list, however, doesn't weave the evidence of the body into a unified whole, and to make things flow for your readers, the body needs to be more unified.

A fake internal pattern seems to be just what you need. Suppose you were to organize the evidence chronologically according to a typical February day. That could provide a clear, recognizable structure for readers (even though it's not really part of the evidence), and it would pull the entire body together. Go ahead and give that a try, and while you're at it, you can also either refocus or delete any of the irrelevant evidence we talked about earlier. Here's what you might end up with:

1. Wake up and look outside: Nature doesn't inspire romance.

    a. Flowers are all dead.

    b. Birds are gone except for the filthy pigeons that eat garbage.

    c. Trees are bare and bleak and depressing.

2. Get up and get dressed for work: Winter clothing is not sexy.

    a. Winter coats make you look fat.

    b. Snow pants make you look fat.

    c. Rubber boots make your feet look stupid.

    d. Long underwear looks unattractive except in the right light and frame of mind.

3. On the way home from work: The weather doesn't turn my thoughts toward love.

    a. It's dark by the middle of the afternoon.

    b. Rain makes me want to cry because it's so tearlike.

4. Alone in my apartment in the evening: Dating seems impossible.

    a. Transportation is difficult.

    b. No new romantic comedies in the theater.

    c. Runny noses are disgusting.

    d. Seeing people kiss makes me think of germs.

Lying in bed that night: All I can do is cry. (This is a larger point illustrated by the next three paragraphs.)

5. I cry in response to the bad weather.

6. I cry in response to the lack of sunlight.

7. I cry in response to sad, February-related news stories.

You have the same list of evidence, with a few deletions, but now it's organized around this fake chronological framework of a typical day in the middle of the most depressing winter of your life. The evidence holds together much more effectively than it did a few pages ago, increasing your odds of achieving flow.

This will be a depressing and far too personal essay for any college class you'll ever take, so I don't recommend you turn it in. File it away under "Future Projects." You can take some comfort, though, in having learned how to make the paragraphs of the body fit together so neatly. That's something. And you have to believe that March will be better. I'm sure it will be.

Chapter Seven

OFFER GOOD EVIDENCE

Because you've planned the body of your essay, writing the rough draft is no longer a matter of figuring out, paragraph by paragraph, what comes next. Now it's only a matter of explaining, paragraph by paragraph, the supporting evidence from your outline. That's a lot easier, and for most student writers, it's a huge relief. Not a few break into quiet song or express their relief with interpretive dance. Writing the rough draft is still hard work, however, so don't get carried away. You need to offer good evidence to your readers, and you need to give credit to the sources of that evidence. That's what you'll look at in this chapter.

Keep in mind, too, that you're still only working on the body of your essay. Openings and closings will have to wait one more chapter. You may not feel great about working on the body of your essay before you've written the opening. That's okay. If your feelings are anything like mine, they don't have the best track record when it comes to guidance.

And your essay doesn't really begin with the opening sentence, does it? It begins with your answer to the question. You then plan out the evidence you'll offer readers to explain and defend your answer, and all of that evidence shows up in the body. So here we are. While it might not feel right to start writing the body before you write the opening paragraph, it's better to draft the body of your essay before you enhance it with a good opening.

EXPLAIN YOUR ANSWER

The first thing to do in the body of your essay is to explain your main idea. That word "explain" often implies that you should defend the idea, too, as in, "Explain yourself, young lady!" In the college essay, this initial explanation is a matter of defining your answer, not defending it. When you developed your writerly thesis statement for this essay, one thing you did was replace vague terms with more precise ones. Now that you're presenting your ideas to readers, your readers need to understand exactly what you mean. So start by defining the key terms of your argument. The defense will come later.

A definition is like a fence. Inside that fence is what you mean by that word. Outside that fence are all the other possibilities. Suppose, for example, that your idea is that fast food is bad food. "Fast food" and "bad food" can mean a lot of different things. Left undefined, they'd require miles of fence to contain all the possible meanings. So if by "fast food" you only mean meals prepared by national hamburger chains, then you better tell that to your readers so they don't get the wrong idea about what to expect inside your fast-food fence. "Bad food" requires an even larger fence for its possible meanings. If by "bad food" you only mean "harmful to the workers who prepare it," then put up a tiny little fence around that word so that your readers won't wonder why all the other possible meanings of "bad food" aren't in your essay.

The definition of your idea should match the evidence you're going to present. If your evidence about fast food is limited to one national chain of restaurants, then you define "fast food" to mean the food from that chain. If your evidence is all about deep-fried foods, then define "fast food" as "anything cooked in a deep fryer." That's a pretty narrow definition of fast food, but if that's where your evidence is, that's where you need to put up your fence. That will tell readers that the many other definitions of "fast food" won't be part of your essay.

You can also define what's inside the fence of your definition by more pointedly stating what's *not* inside the fence. You might suspect, for example, that "fast food" means hamburger chains to a lot of people. If that's not what you mean, then tell your readers to set aside that hamburger-chain definition. Negation can be used anytime, but it's particularly important when your key terms are commonly used to mean something other than what you have in mind.

Examples also help to clarify your definitions. Whether they're hypothetical or personal or historic, they show readers what your definition looks like in real life. If you define "fast food" as anything cooked in four minutes or less, you can then offer a list of possible examples — hamburgers, microwave popcorn, corn dogs, deep-fried pickles, and so on — that help readers see just how broad your definition's boundaries are. Examples are particularly effective when your key terms are abstract. If by "profane" you mean "showing contempt for sacred things," your abstract definition might still be hard for some readers to understand. If you give them an example of what this looks like — spitting on a church, for example — the definition becomes clearer.

Your essay satisfies your readers by living up to the expectations you give them when you first explain your idea. If they know exactly what you mean by your answer to the question, then they also have a more realistic expectation of what evidence they should expect. The narrower boundaries of a precisely defined idea remove from consideration the broad fields of evidence your readers might have otherwise expected from large, undefined terms. The more clearly you define your idea, the better chance you have of satisfying your readers.

OFFER SUMMARIES TO PRESENT YOUR EVIDENCE

As you move on to present the evidence that defends your main idea, you'll need to use summaries to tell your readers the meaning of that detailed evidence. A summary is a statement that compresses a lot of detailed information into a smaller set of words. You can summarize the entire political system of the United States in a single sentence: "The United States is a democratic republic." You can summarize an entire movie — *Casablanca*, for example — with a single word, "predictable."

The value of a summary is its ability to take a large, unwieldy collection of detailed information and package it into a tidy phrase or sentence that tells readers what those details mean.

For most paragraphs, you should use a topic sentence to summarize the detailed evidence it contains. As the first sentence in a paragraph, a topic sentence tells readers what to expect, and the details in the paragraph then satisfy the expectation. If you end with a topic sentence, it summarizes the meaning of all the details that went before it. If you put a topic sentence in the middle of a paragraph, it's usually to show readers how the details before the topic sentence are related to the details that follow. Wherever you place a topic sentence, the effect on your readers is about the same. It satisfies. They sit back and think, Nice paragraph: I see what you mean. Careful readers can still figure out the general idea of a paragraph without a topic sentence, but a good topic sentence will tell careful readers what *you* think the evidence means, and that's important, too.

A topic sentence tells readers what aspect of the main idea you're going to focus on in that paragraph. If your topic sentence says that *Casablanca* is predictable, for example, you've summarized a single quality about the movie. Readers will now expect the details of that paragraph to explain why the plot of the movie is easy to predict. Just as importantly, it also shows readers that you will *not* be looking at the many other characteristics of the movie. That bit of negation might not look like much at first glance. However, getting into all the complexities of *Casablanca* — the dreary cinematography, the inept casting, the annoying way that Humphrey Bogart sucks on his teeth throughout the movie — could take all night. By using the topic sentence to narrow your focus to one smaller point, you can use the paragraph to focus on just that idea with plenty of detailed evidence and not feel guilty for ignoring the rest of this disastrous movie. Not that you'd feel guilty.

Although topic sentences are useful tools, summaries are never sufficient on their own. If you only present a summary and leave out the detailed evidence, you're telling your readers, "Trust me." Some readers might, but careful readers won't. A summary works best when it's backed up by the detailed evidence that it summarizes.

OFFER DETAILED EVIDENCE TO DEFEND YOUR ANSWER

To effectively defend a topic sentence and the main idea it supports, you need to rely on detailed evidence. Details are small pieces of real-world information. They are how things sound, feel, taste, smell, and look. They are the specific prices of items at a grocery store. They are the specific actions — insults shouted, noses bloodied, windows broken — that together become a historical event. They are the actual words of controversial immigration laws, the actual number of killer bees counted by a biologist, the actual length in inches of your belt after a really good Italian dinner. Even if details are made up — as with hypothetical situations — they must be connected to reality by particulars that we *might* see, hear, smell, etc.

Details show readers what your summaries look like in

the real world. Their main work is to establish the objectivity of those summaries and your main idea. However, they also give readers mental images, something that readers can see for themselves with their imaginations. Those mental images are more powerful and interesting than the summaries. Readers love it when their imaginations kick into action. Consider this summarizing sentence: "To keep a relationship healthy, you have to keep it new." That's not terrible as a summary, but left to itself, it's just your opinion, and who are you? To make this idea understood and objective, you have to show readers what you mean with detailed evidence. That might be the facts recorded in a psychological study. It might be a real-world scenario. Here's an example of how you might do the latter:

> With someone you know very well, such as a long-term girlfriend, you might fall into the trap of thinking that there's nothing new for you to learn about her or for her to learn about you. Instead of asking her about her dreams, you ask her to pass the salt. Instead of sharing your fears and desires with her, you share the Metro section of the paper and maybe half of your bagel. Maybe. Gradually, a relationship that used to be full of surprises becomes full of routines and habits and long hours of watching *Law and Order* in silence. It becomes static. It becomes your parents' marriage. But people are always changing — you know that because *you* are always changing — so no matter how well you think you know your long-term girlfriend, you'd be an idiot to think you've learned everything about her. You'd be a bigger idiot to treat the relationship like it was a toaster you paid for a long time ago. To keep a relationship healthy, you have to keep it new.

The details show your readers what you mean by "relationship" and "keep it new." They get the readers' imaginations going, too, because there are particulars here they can visualize. Most importantly, the details demonstrate that such a problem is possible in the real world, that you're not making this up out of thin air. That helps readers take you and what you told them more seriously.

The only unfortunate side effect of giving your readers the detailed evidence they require is that it takes time. Putting detailed evidence into words has a tendency to wear out student writers. After spending long hours assembling precise explanations and paragraph after paragraph of detailed evidence, student writers often tire of their own writing and start to cut out details for fear of boring their readers.

Foolish student writers! Yes, after you spend hours and hours working on detailed evidence, those details may grow dull by familiarity — for you. However, your readers will only spend ten minutes with this same set of details. For your readers, these details aren't boring at all. They show your readers that you've put some thought and research into your essay, that you have a sound basis for your answer to the question. Those details also give your readers something to assemble with their imaginations, and that engages them.

If you don't believe me, try this: Write your essay in advance, set it aside for two days, and then read it. The details that you were sick of two days ago will miraculously become convincing and engaging because the passage of time has changed you from a writer into a reader. On the writer side of the street, yes, the details can wear you out. Familiarity breeds contempt. On the reader side of the street, those same details are great. So hang in there as you show your readers what you mean. If you get tired, take a break. Go bowling. Shop online for shoes. Then come back and finish what you've started.

GIVE CREDIT TO YOUR SOURCES

Academic honesty and professional courtesy require that whenever you use ideas or information from sources outside your own experience or observation, you must tell your readers where the evidence came from. That includes actual words, ideas, stories, information, descriptions — *anything*.

If you don't give credit to your sources, you're guilty of plagiarism, which unfortunately looks like just another vague English-teacher term like "thesis" or "dangling modifier." It sounds like a mild medical condition, a foot rash or inflammation of the elbow. You got plagiarism? No big deal. Put some ice on it. Take an Advil.

That's why I prefer to use a different word for plagiarism. I call it stealing. If you don't give credit to the sources of your information and ideas, you are a thief. You're taking the credit that belongs to another writer and giving it to yourself. Do you remember how you felt about the jerk who broke into your 1986 Honda Civic and stole the car stereo that was worth more than the car itself? That's how you should feel about yourself when you don't give credit to others. It shouldn't feel okay.

The first step in giving credit to your sources is the decision to give credit to your sources. This is a choice you have to make. For that, you're on your own, just you and your conscience. If you and your conscience decide not to do this, however, then you and your conscience might soon be assisted by the Dean of Students and his or her conscience. Even if you feel okay about it, stealing words and ideas remains a serious offense at college, as the Dean of Students will explain.

The second step is learning how to give credit to others. This is what you'll look at in the paragraphs that follow. There's a lot of popular misinformation out there about when and how to give credit to others, so do your best to get rid of any bad ideas you may be harboring and keep in mind the actual principles for crediting outside sources correctly.

GIVE CREDIT EVEN WHEN YOU PARAPHRASE

Contrary to popular belief, you can't just "put it into your own words" and call it good. Putting someone else's ideas into your own words doesn't make those ideas something you thought of. It only obscures who actually deserves credit for the ideas. Whenever you use someone else's ideas in your essay — whether you quote it directly or rephrase it — you must tell your readers whose ideas they are.

One way to do this correctly is to *not* paraphrase. Instead, make a direct, obvious connection between the source of the borrowed words and the actual words you are borrowing. That looks like this:

In a recent letter to the *Itemizer-Herald*, Bill Florence writes, "You people need to stop looking down your noses at Food Mart dining. At my gas station, the corn dogs are *never* more than three days old, and the burritos are updated *daily*."

Regarding the use of torture at the community college, Chickawack Community College's Assistant to the Associate Dean of Instruction, Dr. Robert LeRoy, Ed.D., said that a boring lecture couldn't be considered torture because it "induces rather than deprives a student of sleep."

In these examples, there's no question about which words belong to you and which belong to your outside source. It may seem a little cumbersome to do this properly, but that's okay. You'll get used to it. It's a little cumbersome to do almost anything properly, especially when other people are involved. At some point, you have to either accept that cumbersomeness is a part of life or find yourself eating a lot of microwaved dinners in front of the television.

You can still paraphrase outside ideas and information, of course. In fact, that's what you *should* do with most borrowed evidence, using direct quotations only when the original source is particularly telling or states something exceptionally well. The difference between honest and dishonest paraphrasing is how you give credit to its source. The connection must be just as direct and obvious as it is with a direct quotation:

According to Bill Florence's letter to the *Itemizer-Herald*, the corn dogs at the Texaco Food Mart are always less than four days old and the burritos are always less than two days old.

Chickawack Community College's Assistant to the Associate Dean of Instruction, Dr. Robert LeRoy, Ed.D., denies that boring lectures are torture because there's no sleep deprivation involved.

GIVE CREDIT PRECISELY

Just as paraphrasing is not a legitimate way to avoid giving credit where credit is due, it's also not sufficient to introduce your source and then let your readers guess which evidence came from the source and which came from you. You need to give credit *wherever* credit is due. That means clearly connecting specific sources to the specific ideas or information that you've borrowed.

Are you kidding me? wonder many student writers.

No, I tell them, I'm not kidding. I do not kid.

But I used, like, four sources in one paragraph, they complain, often with pained expressions to underscore their intellectual anguish.

In that case, I tell them, you need to give credit where credit is due, like, four times, sentence by sentence. It looks like this:

> Another threat to sea lions is their increasing addiction to marijuana. In the journal *Science*, J. Ballard provides evidence that bundles of marijuana jettisoned by smugglers have become a favorite meal for sea lions. The *San Diego Union-Tribune* reported that the annual number of reports of stoned sea lions has risen five-fold over the past ten years. This may seem harmless enough, a victimless crime, but a recent study by the Oregon Department of Fish and Wildlife suggests just the opposite. The increasing number of sea lions with "the munchies" has been connected to depleted steelhead runs, the harassment of heavily armed fishing fleets, and the consumption of poisonous three-legged starfish, which according to ranger Jill Rupert, "kind of look like Doritos." All of this puts sea lions at a much greater risk of extinction.

Yes, that is a bit cumbersome. It takes some getting used to.

That's okay, anguished student writer. It's better than stealing from those sources. If most but not all of the information in a paragraph comes from a single outside source, you must clearly distinguish between which material comes from you and which does not. This also means moving through your paragraph sentence by sentence to distinguish your work from the work of others.

You don't need to introduce the single source multiple times, but you do need to refer to it as needed:

> This past November, the *Kansas City Star* reported that beef simply does not taste as good as it used to. According to their exposé, "The Beef with Beef," reporter Van Stavern found that beef, once the king of meats, now regularly loses in taste tests to pork, chicken, and halibut. Stavern also found it mattered little whether the beef in question was cubed, ground, or jerked. This seems hard to believe, but when given this same test, my football-playing, gun-toting brothers all agreed that they preferred a lightly marinated chicken leg to a delicious cheeseburger. This raised an important question for me: Is the quality of the meat changing, or are our tastes changing? The *Star* exposé doesn't answer that question, but this essay will.

Another common error in handling outside ideas or information occurs when students refer vaguely to "studies" as the source of evidence without identifying the titles of the alleged studies or the names of the alleged researchers. Sometimes the studies are obviously made up by dishonest student writers who suppose that a writing professor won't be able to recognize fake information. Little do they know, we sometimes can. More often, however, this vagueness comes from basically honest student writers who can remember the evidence but not the website where they found it. They hope "studies" will be sufficient.

Basically honest but foolish student writers! When this failure of memory occurs — and it occurs all the time — you're faced with three options. One is to use the information, as you remember it, without giving any credit to its forgotten source. This is the easiest thing to do, but it's also lazy and unprofessional. It's *plagiarism* — the impacted bowel of academic disorders! So that's out. The second option is to *not* use the sourceless information. That's ethical, so that's good, but it also weakens your essay. A third option is to go back to the computer or library and track down the actual source of the information so you can give it proper credit. This is the best thing to do, but it takes time and self-discipline. If only you'd been using note cards, this would never have happened. Maybe next time you'll take those note cards more seriously.

One final error to mention is that students will often feel satisfied to put quotation marks around borrowed words, like this:

> Many people think she's a hair fanatic. "Her hair makes you think she's hiding drugs in there, or perhaps a small animal. It's beyond big." It might be wrong to judge someone by how she does her hair, but hair is an important part of the impression a person gives.

The quotation marks are a start because they tell readers that these exact words came from someone other than yourself, but if you don't provide the specific source of those words, the original author hasn't received the credit that's due. It's also distracting. Your readers stop reading your paragraph and start wondering who the author is and where you found the line.

It's better to just name the source, like this:

> Many people think she's a hair fanatic. In a recent *New Yorker* article, Sharon Toland writes, "Her hair makes you think she's hiding drugs in there, or perhaps a small animal. It's beyond big." It might be wrong to judge someone by how she does her hair, but hair is an important part of the impression a person gives.

GIVE CREDIT BEFORE YOU USE EVIDENCE

You should credit to a source before you offer its evidence. If you present the evidence to readers and follow that with a statement of where the evidence came from, you've given credit where credit is due, but you've also given your readers a second or two of confusion. Consider these two examples:

> Used coffee grounds contain traces of ammonia and tannic acid and should never be eaten, even as part of a nationally advertised diet plan. That's according to the Surgeon General.
>
> According to the Surgeon General, used coffee grounds contain traces of ammonia and tannic acid and should never be eaten, even as part of a nationally advertised diet plan.

Both examples say where the borrowed evidence came from, but the second does so without puzzling the readers at any point. Formal documentation systems often allow you to cite your sources immediately after you use their information, but even then your essay will tend to be more readable if you use the source to introduce its information.

GIVE CREDIT WITH ATTRIBUTION

In all of the examples above, you see something that writing professors call "attribution." This is an informal way to give credit to your sources by mentioning a few key pieces of information — often the author, title, and publication — in the body of the essay. Those pieces of information connect your quotation or idea or bit of information to a specific source. They also provide your readers with enough information to allow them to find that source in case they want to learn more or see if you are being honest.

Attribution is a common practice in journalism, where it lives within a fairly complex set of guidelines and standards that we won't get into here. For a journalist, it's sometimes okay to attribute information vaguely ("according to high-level sources") in order to protect the source of that information from retribution. However, even for journalists, it's only okay to be vague like this when you really do have actual sources to protect. In college writing, attribution must always be more precise.

Attribution is a good starting point for giving credit to your sources, so it's often used with short essays, reflection papers, and informal assignments. In addition to the principles you've just read about, effective attribution also requires you to know how to punctuate direct and indirect quotations. If you don't know how to do that, you should take a few minutes to learn the rules for quotation marks.

Punctuation guidelines aren't a part of this book, but they're not hard to find. If you're reading this book as part of a class, you might already own a grammar and punctuation handbook. If so, look up "quotation marks" in the index. If not, ask your professors to recommend a good, cheap handbook. Many professors have a stack of cheap sample handbooks in their offices and will eagerly give you one to encourage your unexpected and delightful interest in punctuation. You can also go to your computer, type "quotation marks" into any Internet search engine, and then work your way through the first five or six listings that have ".edu" in the web address. You'll find what you need.

Give Credit with Formal Documentation

The further you go in your education, the more likely you are to use a system of formal documentation to give credit where credit is due. Most likely, you've run into formal documentation before now. Writers in the humanities — including your writing professors — tend to use and promote a documentation system developed by the Modern Language Association (MLA). The MLA system requires you to mention the author and page number whenever you use evidence in your essay, like this:

In *Call Me Herman*, Melville writes that *Moby-Dick* was never meant to be taken seriously (231).

Moby-Dick was not intended as a philosophical treatise in the form of a whaling novel but "a bunch of hilarious hijinks, just for laughs" (Slemenda 301).

At the end of the essay or term paper, the MLA system asks you to provide a full set of bibliographic information. Here's what that looks like:

Melville, Herman. *Call Me Herman: The Official Autobiography*. Boston: Owl, 1842.

Slemenda, Steve. "Is Melville to be Trusted?" *Journal of Whaling Studies* 39 (2003): 295-308.

This list of works cited in your paper makes it possible for the reader to find and read your sources. The last name and page number you give readers in the body of your paper sends them to the correct listing on the works cited page. They can then use the works cited information to find the source and read it for themselves.

There are several documentation systems out there. Many writers in the social sciences use a system developed by the American Psychological Association (APA). This system requires you to cite the author and date of publication when you borrow evidence from a source. The rest of the source information goes into a bibliography at the end of the essay. Other disciplines use a similar system developed at the University of Chicago. Some science papers put a numbered list of sources at the end of the paper and then cite just the corresponding source number within the body. The documentation system you choose will be the one that's most appropriate for the discipline in which you're writing. It will also be the one your professor tells you to use.

All these systems have two things in common. First, they all cite sources briefly in the body of the paper and provide full bibliographic information elsewhere — footnotes, endnotes, a bibliography page. Second, the details about how to do this are shockingly complex. There's a different way to cite every slightly different type of source — books with one author, books with two authors, books in translation, websites, interviews, newspaper articles, journal articles, articles retrieved from a database, articles cited within a book by Peruvian flute players. To make matters worse, those rules change every three years or so when the scholars in charge of these systems get together to collectively change their minds.

Don't get me wrong. Formal documentation is a good thing. It provides a common set of rules for all students and scholars within a group of disciplines. You can all give credit where credit is due in the same way. This allows everyone to concentrate on the ideas at hand. Even so, learning how to use formal documentation can still be a nightmare.

When it's your turn to learn how to use formal documentation, take a deep breath and then find a good reference guide. For all of these systems, one option is to buy the guide published by that scholarly organization. Most college handbooks also come with abbreviated versions of the guides that are still very good. And you can find what you need online for free at many academic websites, such as Purdue University's Online Writing Lab. Once you find a guide you like, practice using it. That's the main thing to do. What you *shouldn't* do is try to memorize all those rules. That's too much. You'll start having dreams about punctuation and indentation, and according to more than one professional opinion I've received, that's not healthy.

Some professors do fall in love with the intricacies of formal documentation. Be kind to these professors, but do not imitate them. It's essential that you give credit where credit is due and that you do so precisely. Just remember that giving credit, whether by attribution or formal documentation, is not your purpose in writing. It's only one of many writerly tools, like the thesis statement or the topic sentence outline — or note cards. It's here to help you share with others your own thoughtful ideas.

Chapter Eight

GUIDE YOUR READERS

After you've put some time into drafting the body of your essay, the essay can become so familiar that you don't actually see what you've written. For you, the essay exists both as ideas in your brain and as words on the page. When you look at what you've written, you see an essay that makes perfect sense. You see how your evidence defends your main idea. You see how the paragraphs fit together. And if anything *is* missing on the page, your brain fills in that missing piece so that you won't feel bad about screwing up. Your brain loves you.

Your readers, on the other hand, having no direct access to your brain, only see the words that actually made it onto the page. If you left any gaps in your explanations, even small ones, your readers stumble. And even if you presented all the evidence clearly, your readers still won't be as familiar with your essay as you are. From their perspective, the main idea might be hard to figure out. Your evidence, even if it is organized, might appear disorganized or disconnected from a main idea.

Your readers aren't stupid. They just have other things on

their minds — dinners to cook, cars to repair, tedious phone calls from their sisters to try to forget — so they could use a little help when it comes to following your essay. Even your writing professors, who are typically the best readers you'll ever run into, have lives of their own outside the classroom. Most of them, anyway. They might try to patiently unravel your peculiar thought processes and make sense of an incomplete or too-subtle essay, but you can't count on it. So if you want to be understood, you have to treat your readers as if they are a *little* stupid — like people talking on cell phones while they drive. You don't have their full attention.

You have to guide your readers gently through your essay. Make your main idea unavoidably clear in the opening. Point out the organization in the body with fairly obvious transitions. Okay, you tell them. Here comes the second of my four examples. When it's time to wrap things up, you have to give your readers a closing that reminds them about the evidence they just read. Go ahead and mention all the main points of your defense, too, because there's a chance they've already forgotten. Then remind them, one more time, how the body of the essay works together to defend your main idea. After all of that, you also have to check each sentence to make sure there aren't any spelling or punctuation errors to distract your readers.

You need to give your readers far more guidance than you think they need because — this is important — they are not you. For them, this is the first time they've seen your essay. It might be the only time they see it, too. For these distracted readers to understand what they see, it's up to you to guide them safely through your paragraphs.

Use Topic Sentences and Transitions

Your first job is to guide readers through the body of your essay. You understand the different ways in which your paragraphs serve the main idea as examples, reasons, and groups of evidence. You also know how your paragraphs are organized. You can help your readers see how your paragraphs fit together with a few simple tools. We'll start with something familiar.

Use Topic Sentences to Connect Paragraphs

The most direct way to guide your readers though the body of the essay is with topic sentences. You saw in the last chapter how they told readers what to expect from a paragraph. That's part of guiding readers. You can also use topic sentences to show readers how paragraphs connect to your main idea. Suppose, for example, that the main idea of your essay is that gasoline taxes should be raised to pay for solar power development, and suppose this is the current topic sentence for a paragraph:

Generating solar energy will remain expensive using current technology.

That's fine, but you can expand the information in the topic sentence so that it also tells readers how the paragraph connects to your main idea.

If this paragraph explains a reason to raise taxes, you could use this topic sentence:

> Gasoline taxes need to be raised to support solar development in part because generating solar energy will remain expensive using current technology.

This sentence shows readers what evidence will be inside the paragraph (the cost of current technology) and that this is a reason for the main idea (taxes need to be raised to support development).

If the paragraph is related to the main idea by providing some reassurance for doubters of that main idea, you could use this topic sentence:

> These taxes don't have to be permanent because generating solar energy will only be expensive using current technology.

You can also use a topic sentence to show the relationship of one paragraph to another, or to show how a paragraph fits into a larger organizational pattern. Suppose you have a paragraph that presents details about the danger of cigars to one's health. You can use your topic sentence to connect that paragraph to others with references to those others or with transitional words or phrases.

Here are two examples:

> Pipes are okay if you want to die, but cigars are *great*.
>
> Cigars are far less dangerous than cigarettes, and they're less dangerous than chewing tobacco, too, but they will still do their best to kill you.

In both cases, the topic sentence now connects this paragraph to prior paragraphs. In the second example, the topic sentence refers backward to two prior sections and also shows you that the pattern being used is one of decreasing danger.

To improve on your topic sentences, start by making sure your paragraphs have them. You will find, to your horror, that some of your paragraphs are missing topic sentences. "What the — ?" you will say. Don't finish that sentence. Instead, read the offending paragraph closely. Does it have a purpose? If so, add a topic sentence now. That shouldn't be too difficult. If the paragraph doesn't have a discernible purpose, then you need to think about this. Does it need to be edited so that it rejoins the other paragraphs in presenting your main idea? Does it need to be removed? Do what you have to do. If it still has a place in your essay, give it a good topic sentence.

Once your paragraphs are properly outfitted with topic sentences, go back and make those topic sentences better by expanding and rephrasing them so that they connect directly to your main idea or other paragraphs. Don't be bashful about this. Your readers need you to be blunt. That's what kindness looks like in this situation. It's fine to flat-out announce that this paragraph is an example of the main idea or that this next paragraph will present the most compelling reason to accept your idea.

If you lack the courage or good manners to be so obvious, then at least add short phrases to your topic sentences to show how the paragraph is part of a larger idea. You can add phrases that refer backward to past paragraphs — "more importantly," "another example," "a bigger mistake" — or forward to future paragraphs. You can repeat key words or phrases from your main idea to remind your readers about that idea. Do *something*. Your topic sentences long to live more fulfilling lives in your essay.

USE TRANSITIONS TO POINT OUT RELATIONSHIPS AND ORGANIZATION

Transitions, whether they are sentences, phrases, or words, help readers see how the parts of the essay fit together. They might point out the relationship of two or three items, as in a list, or they might point out the organization of the essay.

Transitional statements are usually single sentences found at the beginning and end of subsections of the essay. They might be topic sentences, or they might act like topic sentences for multiparagraph sections of the essay. At any pivotal point in the essay, you can also use a transitional paragraph to explain how the writing that follows is related to the writing that went before it. Here's a transitional statement that is also a topic sentence:

> Before one can understand the full effects of addiction to high-fructose corn syrup, it is important to first understand the chemical makeup of this seemingly benign substance.

This transition does two things. The first half prepares the reader for a broader set of paragraphs that examine the full effects of this addiction. That tells us what we can now expect in the coming paragraphs. The second half introduces the chemical analysis of corn syrup and suggests that it's not so benign. That tells us that we can now expect some detailed evidence about this point in the paragraph.

Here are examples of transitional statements that might show up later in this particular essay:

> So much for the chemical makeup — what about the effects of these chemicals on the user?
>
> Dehydration is only the first and least consequential effect, and more troubling is the rapid rise in heart rate.
>
> As if these effects weren't bad enough, high-fructose corn syrup also leads to dangerous levels of hyperactivity that renders the "syrup-sucker" useless as a human being.
>
> The worst effect, however, is the drawn-out depression that follows the use of high-fructose corn syrup, a depression that grows deeper and more difficult to escape with each round of syrup-sucking.
>
> With effects this severe, why are kids today turning from traditional recreational drugs to high-fructose corn syrup?

These statements might seem a little obvious when pulled out of paragraphs and listed like this. They are. They should be. As your essay gets longer and gives your readers more to think about, obvious statements like these become less obvious and more helpful. Collectively, this group of transitions helps readers see both a cause and effect pattern and a least-to-most harmful pattern within the paragraphs. The repetition of the key term "syrup-sucking" reminds readers, again and again, that this is the topic of the essay. That's exactly what your distracted readers need to put together the pieces of your essay.

Transitional phrases and words work like transitional statements, but they do so within sentences instead of standing on their own as independent sentences or paragraphs. They are easy and effective additions to topic sentences, and you can use them within your paragraphs. Some transitional phrases show how ideas are logically related to each other as additions or examples or contrasting thoughts. Here's an example of how transitions (in bold) work within a paragraph:

> **When you finally come to the end of your excuses,** the only option left is to look at your mistake **and then** admit that you blew it. My mother calls this "the point of no return." **When you finally arrive at the point of no return,** you're **not only** willing to admit your mistake **but also** to abandon it. **For example,** you admit that **in the past** you were petty about splitting expenses exactly down the middle. You shouldn't have asked her to pay for half of a beer from which she only took a sip. That was dumb. **In the future,** you won't do that. You will **instead** be generous. You **also** admit that **in the past** you were maybe a little harsh in your comments about her appearance. You didn't need to ask if she was retaining water or just putting on weight. That was dumb *and* mean. **In the future,** you won't make those comments, even if you're seriously wondering. **In the future,** you'll be kind. **When you finally get to the point of no return,** it may be too late to save a relationship, **but** you can at least move forward toward a healthier future **by** not returning to those kinds of stupid mistakes.

These shorter transitions refer either to the pattern of organization for the essay ("even worse," "in the past," "in the future") or link two ideas with a word or two of transition or sequence ("however," "for example," "but," "not only"). The repetition of key terms also helps us to remember the topic and purpose of this paragraph.

Transitional words and phrases don't stand out as much as full transitional sentences, but they still do a good job of helping your readers see how smaller pieces of explanation fit together. You should use them *a lot*. Even when they seem to draw attention to themselves — as with all the "in the future" and "in the past" repetition — what they are actually drawing attention to is the organization (before and after) and the main point (change over time), making it more likely that your reader will see this. It's hard to overdo it with transitions.

GIVE YOUR READERS AN EFFECTIVE OPENING

Once the body of your essay is complete, it's time to write the opening and closing — finally. You remember the openings from your old friend, the five-paragraph trainer-essay. For that opening, you used some kind of catchy hook to introduce the topic ("According to Webster, a 'catastrophe' is 'something that is catastrophic.' That certainly describes my recent trip to Iowa."), and you followed it with your thesis statement ("Never vacation in Iowa because of the heat, the humidity, and the profuse sweating."). Would you be surprised if I told you this kind of opening is no longer sufficient?

With almost any kind of writing, the opening has two jobs. First, it should engage your readers' interest. Second, it must show readers what to expect. With the college essay, engaging your readers' interest is a little trickier to understand. On the one hand, your readers, most of the time, are professors who are paid to read your essays, so read them they will whether you engage their interest or not. You just don't want to set up barriers for them with *dis*engaging openings like the one above. On the other hand, you'll share many of your essays with other students. They will need more engagement than your professors. With both of these potential readers, however, the more important job for the college essay opening is to clearly let those readers know what to expect.

Here are a few standard opening techniques that you can use to mildly engage your readers and let them know what to expect.

THE BIG PICTURE

Readers usually enjoy seeing the big picture before you zoom in to present a narrower question and your main idea. Providing some context shows your readers that your topic is part of something larger, and that you're aware of this. It acknowledges the limitations of your essay, too, which is a good thing. It shows readers that you're only going to concentrate on one part of the big picture and that you're doing this intentionally, not accidentally. Here's an example:

> The two-party political system has been a part of the American scene since before there was a true sense of what "the American scene" was. It hasn't always been Republicans and Democrats, of course, but it has always been two main parties. Whenever a third party has arisen for one reason or another — the Bull Moose Party of Teddy Roosevelt's time or the Republican Party of the mid-1800s — the third party either gained

enough power to displace one of the previous major parties or it faded away to become one more footnote in American history. With so many problems present in our current political mess, it's no wonder that reform parties are making headway in their efforts to enter this political system. However, the question remains as to the long-term viability of today's minor parties.

In this opening, the author discusses the two-party situation and then zooms in on the one part of this topic, whether a modern third party could make it in the American political system. If you have an interest in politics, or perhaps if you're curious to learn that there weren't always Republicans, this might get your brain curious about why this is so.

You'll notice that you don't get a readerly thesis statement with this opening. The readerly thesis statement is not the monster sentence you wrote as part of deciding on the best answer to your question. The readerly thesis statement is a streamlined sentence that captures the main idea briefly and, I would hope, elegantly. You don't find one in this opening, but the opening still works because readers don't need to know the main idea yet. They only need to know what the topic is and what sort of main idea they can expect.

ANECDOTES

An anecdote is a brief story that uses a personal experience, hypothetical situation, historical incident, or other event to introduce your topic. This is popular because stories are easy to remember and they show how an idea works in the real world. Whether you use real-life anecdotes or invented ones makes little difference to your readers. Stories are stories. You can also start with just half of an anecdote and save the other half for your closing. Here's an example of an anecdote at work:

> When I was twenty-two, I shot myself. It happened while I was cleaning out my uncle's trailer. He'd been using the drawer of his bedside table for an ashtray, and when I dumped the cigarette butts into the garbage can, I found that he'd also been using it as a gun locker. His handgun went off when it landed in the garbage can, and the bullet passed through my calf and out through the wall.
>
> I was lucky, but many others aren't. Thousands of family members die every year because of these weapons. Don't get me wrong about handguns. In spite of what happened to me, I remain ready to defend the right of every American to own handguns. But these handguns should come with one simple safety feature that will keep them from putting family members at risk: removable triggers.

In this two-paragraph opening, the first paragraph tells the anecdote, and the second paragraph transitions from that anecdote to an introduction of the topic and main idea. Spending so much time engaging the readers makes this a little more informal than most academic essays need to be, and it might get some complaints from some fussy professors. At the same time, those same fussy professors might not realize yet how tired they are of colorless, to-the-point openings. An opening like this might thus be quite effective. You just have to be careful about whether it's appropriate for a particular audience.

This opening does include a readerly thesis statement. It's the last sentence of the second paragraph. This sentence doesn't capture the full complexity of the essay's idea — that's the job of the *writerly* thesis statement, the one you write for your eyes only — but it does briefly state the main point that the rest of the essay will explain and defend.

TEXTUAL REFERENCES AND QUOTATIONS

When your topic is a text of any sort, good manners and professional courtesy require you to introduce the author and title of the text early in your opening, like this:

> In Willa Cather's *My Ántonia*, the narrator . . .

Besides this obligatory introduction of the general topic, you will also do well to focus your readers' attention on some relevant quotation or illustration from the text itself that will show readers what to expect from your essay.

Here's an example:

> In Willa Cather's *My Ántonia*, the narrator, Jim Burden, makes a big deal about every little thing he remembers. Looking back on his childhood experience of arriving on the Nebraska frontier in the middle of a moonless night, he writes: "There was nothing but land: not a country at all, but the material out of which countries are made.... Between that earth and that sky I felt erased, blotted out. I did not say my prayers that night: here, I felt, what would be would be." It's understandable that this would be a bold memory for a young boy to carry, but would that boy be wrestling with the big questions of existence while on that wagon ride or would he simply be trying to keep from falling out of the wagon? That leads us to another and more important question: Just how far can we trust this narrator?

This sort of an essay might not be your cup of tea. In fact, you might need a cup of coffee if you're not a fan of American literature. However, you can see that the opening does a good job of introducing the topic — the narrator of Willa Cather's novel — and that it uses this passage to introduce an important question about his reliability. You don't get a thesis statement, but you still know what to expect from the essay.

Textual references aren't limited to essays about texts. They can be used with any topic. You might use them to illustrate an idea in the same way you would use an anecdote:

> When Huck Finn finally gets some money at the end of Mark Twain's novel *Huckleberry Finn*, he is able to handle civilization for about a month and then says it's time to "light out for the territories." He disappears from view, never to be seen again. During the last decade, thousands have followed Huck Finn in his flight to the territories. These are young professionals who have amassed small fortunes in a few short years as stockbrokers, software engineers, and baristas. Suddenly they realize they find no pleasure in material gain, and they slip away to Alaska, Idaho, or New Jersey, never to be seen again. They are looking for something else, something just beyond their grasp. But here's a little secret: They won't ever find that elusive something else in "the territories." Huck Finn never found it. Nobody ever does.

In this example, the quotation introduces the topic of "lighting out for the territories." The author then shows how this continues in current times and presents the main idea of the essay — that neither financial success nor escape to "the territories" is the "something else" that so many of us are looking for. The reference to *Huckleberry Finn* is only here to get us started. This will not be an essay about Twain's novel.

OTHER TECHNIQUES

In addition to these major techniques, you have a couple of other options that don't usually stand on their own as openings but may still be useful when used with other strategies.

Humor is not common in academic writing because academics are generally humorless. That means you won't get away with much of it. However, a *little* humor slipped in quietly can make an opening more engaging for readers, even if they don't quite understand why. That was good, thinks your biology instructor, not realizing that what she likes about your opening is the way you introduce the topic of frog eggs by explaining how they have the texture and *taste* of Gummi bears. In academic writing, a little humor goes a long way. Anything more than that goes *too* far.

Questions are another useful device. If you ask a question that readers are curious about, it engages that curiosity. Just make sure you eventually answer any questions you raise — even if your answer is that this particular question has no easy answer. There's nothing worse than asking a great question and then denying your readers the satisfaction of a great response. That's like asking a friend, "You remember that twenty bucks I borrowed?" and then adding, "I still don't have it. Ha ha." It's not good for the relationship.

GIVE YOUR READERS AN EFFECTIVE CLOSING

One good thing about writing the body first and the opening and closing later is that you might actually write a closing. When student writers start with the opening and then write the body, they seem to wear out by the end of the body. Having said all they really need to say in the body, they scribble down the barest of closings and quit. They become long-distance runners who sit down with ten yards to go and tell the cheering fans, "You get the point. I more or less ran the entire race."

Foolish student writers! Are you tired? Take a nap. Then come back and tell your readers about the triumph that is the body of your essay. Remind them of your main points. Remind them about how those points work together to defend your idea. Speaking of your main idea, remind them of that, too. Restate it. Tell them, in a polite way, what they can do with it.

Although you're right to think that the body of a good essay has said everything that needs to be said, your distracted readers need more than that. Detailed evidence defends your idea clearly and effectively, but reading a lot of detailed evidence all at once can be overwhelming. To guide your readers through to the end of your essay, your closing has to summarize that evidence and briefly remind readers how the evidence adds up to defend your main idea. The closing should also emphasize that idea one last time. Everyone needs closure. I can tell you that from personal experience.

The closing doesn't have to be long. It just has to be complete. Here's a single closing that's only a paragraph long but still wraps things up effectively:

> Who then should bear the blame for this catastrophe? The evidence is clear enough. Delvin Baird hired the uncertified electrician who installed the overhead lava lamps. Delvin Baird never scheduled the electrical inspection that would have shown that the overhead lava lamps were defective and dangerous. Delvin Baird removed the sprinkler system without any mention of this to his clients, even though he met with them 14 times after this decision. Only one person is to blame for what happened on November 13: Delvin Baird.

The repetition of the villain's devilish name is the only writerly device the author uses here. It reminds us of the topic of the essay. Otherwise, this is a simple summary of the main points of evidence. It's followed by an equally simple restatement of the main idea. That's long enough. It does its job.

If you want to wrap things up more colorfully, that's fine, too, as long as you still do the more important work of summarizing your evidence and emphasizing your main idea. You have many options for adding color to your closings, just as you have many options for openings. Anecdotes are popular. You can also bring in textual references and quotations. In addition to these favorites, you might try two other techniques that are only used with closings — the second half of an anecdote and the call to action.

THE SECOND HALF OF AN ANECDOTE

You set up this technique by telling the first half of an anecdote in the opening of your essay. That gives them some motivation to continue reading — to find out how the story ends. At the end of the essay, you reward them with the second half of the opening anecdote. Here is a closing that provides the second half of the anecdote:

> What happened to Wild Bob? Unfortunately, Wild Bob's story ended like that of many others who suffer from TF. He lost his job because of the safety risks he posed. His family was driven away. Finally he gave up, sealed the air vents in his room, and let the disease run its course. Wild Bob's story illustrates how desperate life can be for victims of TF.
>
> As you've seen, however, ongoing research suggests that relief is on the way. Friesen and Friesen's identification of the "TF gene" is a step toward long-term eradication. Dr. Libby's research with saliva builds on their efforts, opening the door to the gene therapy proposed by Dylan in her groundbreaking paper. In the short term, the Beeler Foundation's "smelling nose" cats offer immediate help, as does the Cooper brothers' creative use of water filtration technology. And let's not forget Richardson's astonishing results with therapeutic bowling, suggesting that a solution might be found with simple lifestyle changes.
>
> As this promising medical research suggests, we can soon write a new ending for the TF story. For that to happen, the research must move forward. This is why Congress must renew its funding for the TF Institute. The results of current work are too promising to be ignored. For all the Wild Bobs out there, continued funding is a matter of life and death.

This closing starts by giving readers some resolution with the sad ending of the Wild Bob anecdote. It follows that with a thorough summary of the evidence from the body. The last paragraph then connects both Wild Bob and the summarized evidence to the main idea — keep the money coming because the research is making progress. This ending is too long for a short essay, but it's just right for a longer paper that has presented a lot of detailed evidence.

A CALL TO ACTION

The call to action builds a bridge between the main idea and your readers by giving them practical ways to make the main idea a part of their lives. If a call to action is appropriate for your main idea, it comes with several advantages. Each action you call for is an application of your main idea to real-life situations. More importantly, it makes your idea tangible for your readers. If they see how your idea connects to their lives, they understand your idea more clearly. The only weakness is that, on its own, a call to action doesn't summarize the details in the body and connect them to the main idea. That's easy to fix, though. You summarize the evidence and then call your readers to action. Here's an example:

> Unfortunately, ending the practice of clear-cutting is more easily said than done. The majority of private forests are now held by huge timber corporations, and short-term profit is their primary goal. The majority of public forests are managed by government agencies that see our forests as agricultural crops. These factors make it hard for the average person to influence forest practices directly. However, there are three easy, effective things to do to indirectly remove clear-cutting as a widespread forest-management practice:
>
> 1. Use less timber. Buy recycled wood products such as OSB sheet-

ing, HardiPlank siding, and decking made from plastic and recycled wood. These alternatives are becoming more common and can be found at most building supply stores.

2. Make your priorities known to your current political representatives with letters and email. They won't know you're unhappy unless you tell them, and they are savvy enough to know when the tide has finally turned.

3. Vote for politicians who care more about ecological forests than corporate profits. They are out there, and in increasing numbers.

We can make a difference. We just have to take some first steps and encourage others to join us in doing the same. The rest will follow.

This is a lengthy closing, too, and again, that's okay as long as the body of the essay also takes its time laying out the details of its evidence. In this example, you have a writer who knows that the body of the essay is solid and is now taking a little victory lap. Good for you, victorious student writer.

DON'T DISTRACT YOUR READERS

Sentences and formatting are the most superficial elements of a college essay. They form the actual physical product that readers hold in their hands and read. You might think that presentation doesn't matter compared to the ideas and evidence of your essay, and in a way, you'd be right — your essay has to be good thinking first. However, presentation still matters a lot. If your essay looks good, some readers will look at it and assume that the thinking is good, too. And many will take you more seriously when they see you know your way around a sentence or that you're an old pro with MLA formatting.

The bigger issue, though, is that errors on the surface of the essay distract readers from your ideas. If your sentences are confusing, all that hard work you put into the thinking loses its value. If your essay doesn't follow required format guidelines, some fussy professors might not even read it. So the final way to guide your distracted readers through your essay is to remove any obstacles in your presentation that might cause them to stumble.

FOLLOW ASSIGNMENT GUIDELINES

Start with the format of your essay. If the assignment requires formal documentation, it also requires the formatting rules for that documentation system — margins, page numbering, allowable font sizes, and so on. These rules are detailed and thorough, but it's nothing you can't handle. Use the guide in that handbook of yours.

If the assignment requires no formal documentation, it's still a good idea to follow formatting rules. That makes you look good as a serious student, and it makes your essay more readable. If you set your elegantly formatted essay down next to the handwritten essay of another student, you'll see what I mean. So will the other student. Yours will look more intelligent, even if it's not.

Your professor might add other rules beyond formatting. You might need to stay within minimum and maximum length requirements. You might need to use a minimum number of sources. Don't think of these rules as suggested guidelines. Think of them as felonies you'd rather not commit. Don't add avoidable, superficial problems to your essay.

WRITE GOOD SENTENCES

The most serious distractions in college writing are sentence-level mistakes that college writers are expected to avoid with proper spelling, usage, punctuation, and grammar.

I understand, grammatically challenged student writer, that all of these technicalities were taught when you were in fifth grade, and that the only thing you now remember from fifth grade is the afternoon your sister Nadine busted you for smoking cigarettes in the attic with Mike Stradley and Steve Rayner. I understand how totally not fair it is that now, after all these misspent years, you are expected to write proper sentences.

Unfortunately, that gross unfairness doesn't change anything. You are now responsible for your sentences, and that's just the way it goes. As my mother used to tell me, Don't be a ninny — if life was fair, would I be stuck here listening to you whine all afternoon?

My point is that if you have any problems writing grammatical sentences, as you almost certainly do, it's time for you to work on these technical skills so that your readers will be able to see your wonderful ideas and not your terrible sentences. This might take some work, but it's rewarding work. It builds confidence. And if you've been doing any reading at all since fifth grade, your technical skills are probably better than you think.

It's beyond the scope of this little book to offer much direct help. You probably only need to work on four or five things, but they could be any four of five things from a list of a hundred possibilities. For that kind of problem, you need a more individualized kind of treatment. If you have a writing professor, and if your writing professor has not already told you what to work on, ask your writing professor what to work on. If you don't have a writing professor but attend a school with the good sense to fund a writing center, use that excellent resource.

If you're on your own, you can use an Internet search engine to search for information about commas. That's a good starting point. How did I know you needed to work on commas? Because *everyone* needs to work on commas. Everyone was taught to put a comma wherever you would take a breath, and that is one of the worst rules of thumb ever. Commas are related to the meaning of your sentence, not the size of your lungs. Learn to follow comma rules and you'll fix at least one of your problems.

From there, you might find a used grammar handbook and start reading through it, a few pages at a time. This is not engaging reading, but those handbooks cover everything, so reading through one will refresh your memories of fifth grade, minus the cigarette incident, and help you to identify the rules of usage and punctuation that you don't remember anymore.

I can also tell you one thing to *not* do. Do not trust software to fix your punctuation and spelling errors. You're just asking for trouble. Spelling errors are bad, but spell-*checking* errors are worse. A spell-checking error occurs when your software tells you that you've misspelled a word — which is fine

— and then suggests a correctly spelled word to replace it. This is where the trouble occurs. If you don't look up the meaning of that suggested word, you might easily accept a very distracting suggestion.

One of my colleagues showed me an example. A student meant to write this: "I tried to insinuate myself into the conversation." The student misspelled "insinuate," however, and then blindly accepted the advice of his software. The sentence became this: "I tried to inseminate myself into the conversation." That's hard to do.

These spell-checking errors are great fun for writing professors. We send them around to each other and yuk it up at your expense. But they also ruin otherwise good essays by distracting readers so powerfully. So use the spell-checker to find misspellings, but also use a dictionary to look up the meanings of your alternatives before you accept them.

Grammar checking software is even worse, by the way. The last time anyone *really* needed a semicolon was June of 1908, so turn down those semicolon suggestions. Turn down any grammar-related suggestions. Turn that feature off, in fact. If you can't tell the difference between a sentence that makes sense and one that doesn't, software isn't going to solve the problem. You instead need a few points of theory and some individualized help to recognize how those grammatical theories work in your own writing. So go to your writing professor, or your college writing center, or a good thick handbook of grammar to get started. It's not that complicated, but you do need to understand actual ideas about grammar. You need to stop guessing.

PROOFREAD ONE LAST TIME

The last way to gently guide your readers is to proofread your work one last time for any superficial errors that might distract them. Even if your sentence-making skills need some improvement, you can still proofread your work to make sure each sentence makes sense on its own. The problem, as we've already seen, is that your brain knows what's *supposed* to be on the page, so that's what your lying eyes will probably see when they proofread, whether or not it's really there.

To proofread your work, then, you have to read your essay as if you hadn't written it. You have to look at it from your readers' perspective. That's not easy, especially if you're working on your own, but there are ways to do this. The best way is to finish the essay a day or two before the deadline and set it aside. Then come back to it later and see what you think. You'll be amazed. It won't be the same essay. Your brain will have moved on to other tasks, so if you left out the word "not," you'll notice that now. Similarly, if you misspelled a word or used "comma" instead of "coma," you'll see that now and fix it.

If you don't have that kind of time, you can ask someone to read your paper to you. That puts you in the place of the audience by turning your essay into a spoken thing that is entirely outside of your brain. This also helps you identify sentences that don't make sense. Whenever your reader stumbles, stop the reader and fix the sentence. If you have no one around who is willing to read your essay to you, read it out loud to yourself. That's not as good, but it's better than reading it silently. When you read it out loud, it's harder for your brain to trick you into thinking that everything's fantastic.

If you know that you have trouble with ungrammatical sentences, then even before you learn all the rules for writing good sentences, you can read your essay backward, sentence by sentence, and make sure each sentence stands on its own as a complete idea. That's one functional test for grammatical sentences. This is also a good way to identify sentence fragments that sometimes make sense when their meaning depends on a prior sentence. Like this one. You still need to work on your technical understanding of how sentences work, but reading your essay backward will help for the time being.

One more thing to remember is that proofreading should be the last thing you do with your essay before you print it on clean white paper and put a triumphant staple through the upper left corner. You've worked from the inside out to build this essay, starting with your main idea and then adding the body paragraphs that explain and defend it. From there, you worked on the opening and closing. You added transitions and improved your topic sentences. That was a lot of work, but now that work is done.

As a proofreader, you're just trying to locate and smooth out clunky phrases or missing words or misplaced commas. This is last-minute dusting so that your readers won't be slowed down by even minor distractions as they follow the ideas in your essay. You're winding down, so try not to get wound up over all the other paragraphs you could have written for this essay. This won't be the last essay you ever write.

Part Four

IMPROVING YOUR ARGUMENT

The first three parts of the book have introduced you to argument and the college essay. If you've been paying attention, you should now understand the basics of how to develop an essay that presents an opinion of your own and defends your opinion with appropriate evidence.

That's a good accomplishment, but in these final chapters, you'll learn how to write better essays with reasons, with improved credibility, and with more sophisticated models for presenting an argument. You'll also learn what the word "essay" really means, so stick around.

Chapter Nine

OFFER GOOD

REASONS

The most important kind of defense for an argument is direct evidence — facts from the real world that show how your argument makes sense in reality. If you have enough direct evidence, you don't need to worry about reasons. You just lay down those facts like a lawyer laying down glossy photographs from the scene of the crime. The only problem is that you almost never have enough direct evidence to defend your main idea. In fact, that's often what makes a question debatable — there's not enough direct evidence, so people disagree about the answer.

That's where reasons come in.

Reasons are not facts. Like your main idea, reasons are opinions of yours. The difference is that instead of answering questions directly, reasons explain why your main idea is a good answer. They're like an entourage of defenders for your main idea. If your main idea has enough direct evidence, it doesn't need an entourage. But without sufficient direct evidence, your answer needs reasons to defend itself.

Suppose you tell your former girlfriend that you might kind of miss her. Think of that as the main idea of an argument. She responds by telling you to prove it. You realize you should have thought this through a little more because you don't really have any direct evidence to offer. Nonetheless, you offer a reason — an idea of your own — to defend your main idea. Well, you say, I miss you because you're friendlier than the cat. That's not a very good reason, but it's a reason. Her level of friendliness relative to the cat is an opinion of yours, not a fact, and it does help to explain why you miss her.

Suppose she has doubts about the validity of this reason. You can then defend your reason with real-world evidence — and regarding the unfriendliness of the cat, you have plenty of evidence. So now the evidence defends the reason, and the reason, bolstered by that evidence, defends your main idea. The defense of the main idea still depends on real-world evidence. It either supports the main idea directly or, as in this case, it supports the main idea indirectly by supporting a reason.

In this chapter, you'll look first at arguments that don't need reasons — those are the kind of arguments you've been studying so far. Then you'll look at how reasons work and how to use them sensibly. You'll see that reasons are useful throughout the writing process. When you gather evidence, for example, you can look for facts that are directly relevant to your question and possible answers but also indirectly relevant to possible reasons for an answer. When you decide the best answer to your question, you can base that decision on direct evidence and on reasons that are supported by indirect evidence. As you present your answer to others, you can offer reasons now, too.

WHEN YOU DON'T NEED REASONS

For some essays, you don't need reasons because you have sufficient evidence that's directly related to your question. Usually, if there's enough real-world evidence to answer a question convincingly, people already agree on an answer and don't need to argue. In some cases, however, the direct evidence is out there, but people disagree about the patterns or meanings of that evidence. In those cases, you can build an argument about what you think the evidence means and then defend that answer with the evidence itself.

This kind of argument is called an **inductive argument**. It looks at a collection of detailed evidence and from that evidence draws a general conclusion about what it means or how it works. This inductive type of thinking is the process you've used to teach yourself almost everything you know. You were hungry, so you cried, and people fed you. You observed that pattern a few thousand times and arrived at the conclusion that crying is magic. The evidence told you that if you cry, people feed you. And so they did until you turned two. This is also how you learned the meaning of words. It's how you learned to ride a bike. It's how you've figured out almost everything that you've ever figured out.

Induction is great for navigating the world, but you can sometimes defend a main idea with it, too. In the world of politics, for example, you have arguments based on polling. Polling is the process by which researchers gather direct evidence from people. Researchers might ask whether people are likely to vote for a candidate or to what degree they approve or disapprove of a person or policy. The principles of successful polling are quite complex, and there's math involved, so we won't try to explain it in any detail. In short, though, good polls are able to extract credible evidence from the minds of a small number of would-be voters and from that evidence draw direct conclusions about broader public attitudes and political outcomes. Those conclusions are opinions — interpretations of the data. The polling data is evidence. There's a direct connection between the two, so no reasons are required to defend those assertions and predictions.

Similarly, in the world of law, physical evidence can be used to directly defend an opinion. In a legal argument, the main idea is often whether a person's behavior does or does not fit the definition of a crime. The definition of "burglary," for example, usually requires three elements: 1) breaking into a structure, 2) entering the structure, and 3) intending to commit a crime. To convict someone of burglary, then, a prosecutor must provide direct evidence of all three ingredients.

When I was in high school, a friend and I broke into the high school gym so we could play basketball. When the cops showed up, guns drawn, they quickly gathered direct evidence for two out of the three parts of the burglary definition. We had used my student body card to jimmy open the door, and we had walked inside. That was direct evidence of breaking and entering. However, our intent was to shoot baskets, which is not a crime, so we did not meet that part of the burglary definition. We still had to sit in the back of a cop car for two hours, and we were suspended from school for trespassing, but at least we could tell our parents that we weren't burglars. They were glad to hear that.

In academic writing, questions about literary texts or world events or some scientific issues might offer enough direct evidence for you to draw a conclusion about what it all means. In Arthur Miller's *Death of a Salesman*, for example, you can ask whether Willy Loman is a true tragic hero. To answer that question, you define "true tragic hero" and then look at the evidence from Miller's play to see whether the patterns in Willy Loman's actions fit that definition. Or, you might ask if major league baseball players have more serious injuries than major league soccer players. Define what you mean by "serious injuries" and then start looking for evidence about these athletes. If you can find patterns of injuries in a large enough pool of athletes, you can answer the question with direct evidence rather than reasons.

You won't often use induction as the main defense in an essay, however. Most of your debates are over questions where the direct evidence is lacking — questions about the future, questions about why things happened, questions about what should be done, questions about the meaning of insufficient evidence. For those questions, you need reasons.

HOW REASONS WORK

Reasons are ideas that explain why your main idea is a good one. They might be widely accepted observations or wild opinions, but for your reasons to be effective, they must be relevant to your main idea, they must be credible, and they must be logical.

Suppose, for example, that your sister calls you an idiot. That is her main idea, and I'll assume that it's an opinion rather than a fact. You ask her why she says so. She gives you her reason — because you let Denise, your former girlfriend, "get away." Let's check this defense for relevance first.

Main Idea: You are an idiot.

Reason: You let Denise get away.

A reason is relevant when it's an idea about the same topic as your main idea. In this case, both the main idea and the reason are opinions about you, so this is a relevant reason.

Is this reason credible? Let's suppose it's true that you let your girlfriend get away, possibly by being unappreciative of the value she added to your otherwise drab life, so much so that she eventually grew tired of your whining and moved out of your apartment and into your mother's house — which you know is very weird, but you're not going to get into that. So yes, then, the reason is also credible.

Is the reason logical?

"Logical" is a broad term that can mean many things in many different situations. In this situation, the term refers to a type of thinking called **deduction**. Deduction is not the opposite of induction, but it works very differently. With induction, you start by looking at lots of particular pieces of evidence and then, from these particulars, you draw a general conclusion about what that evidence means — the power of crying, the meaning of "dog," and so on. With deduction, you take a general idea and apply that general idea to a particular situation with your reason. Induction taught you the general idea that crying gets you fed. With deduction, you apply that general idea to a particular situation: Mom will give me a cookie because I am crying (and people feed me when I cry).

When it comes to your reasons, then, "logical" means that the general idea behind that reason is also appropriate for this situation and a credible idea on its own. Here's what that looks like with the Denise argument:

Main Idea: You are an idiot.

Reason: You let Denise get away.

Underlying General Idea: Only an idiot would let someone like Denise get away.

So is the reason logical? To test that, we have to test the underlying general idea. It's a general idea about what an idiot would do regarding Denise. So yes, it passes the first test of logic. It's appropriate for the situation. Is the underlying general idea credible? More and more, I'm starting to think so. So yes, it seems to pass the second test. Because the underlying general idea is appropriate to this situation and credible, the reason is logical. Oh well.

With deduction, by the way, the terms of the argument often go by different names, like this:

Claim: You are an idiot.

Reason: You let Denise get away.

Assumption: Only an idiot would let someone like Denise get away.

It makes sense to call your main idea a claim because you're claiming that it is true, that this is the best available answer to the question. Changing "general underlying idea" to "assumption" also makes sense because the assumption is usually an idea that you assume your audience will accept as credible, an idea you won't have to defend. If the assumption is an idea that your audience might disagree with, then it's important to either defend the assumption as well or find another reason that comes with a more agreeable assumption.

How can someone transform this three-part set of ideas into an actual presentation? In a conversation with your big sister, the flow of ideas and evidence is hard to chart, especially if your sister offers a claim when it's raining and you're standing there holding a fairly heavy bag of kitty litter for the stupid cat that super-fantastic Denise left behind. However, if your sister goes home and writes her argument down in a lengthy and totally unnecessary email, her deductive argument might be structured like this:

Claim: I know you don't want to hear this, but you're still an idiot.

Reason: You really did let Denise get away.

Evidence: You stopped taking her out, you stopped asking her questions about herself, you were petty about finances, you complained
all the time about college administrators, you made her proofread
all your poems, etc., until she didn't think you cared about her at all.

Assumption: Only an idiot would let someone like Denise get away.

Evidence: Denise is awesome — hilarious, creative, generous, and
too smart to be taken for granted. Only an idiot would *not* work hard
to maintain a healthy relationship with someone so great.

Notice that none of the evidence is *directly* related to the
question of your intelligence. There's nothing here about IQ
tests, for example, or how well you did on your SAT exams.
Instead, the evidence is all directly connected to the reason —
that you let an awesome girlfriend get away — and the assumption — that only an idiot would do something like that. The
evidence defends the reason and its assumption. Those ideas
then work together to defend the main idea that you are an
idiot. That's how deductive arguments work, both in real-life
situations like the one above and, with some adjustments, in
academic writing.

TEST YOUR REASONS

In an academic paper, you might offer several reasons that
defend your main idea. These should be good reasons, so that
means testing the three qualities of a good reason to make sure
that it is relevant, credible, and logical. In a deductive argument, the boldness of your claim — your main idea — should
be equal to the strength of your reasons.

In Act 5 of *Hamlet*, for example, Hamlet jumps into his former girlfriend's grave and tells her grieving brother that "forty thousand brothers" couldn't have loved Ophelia as much as he did. Really, Hamlet? Forty thousand brothers? Hamlet's assertion raises the question of just how strongly Hamlet actually loved Ophelia. It's a question you can't answer inductively because there's zero direct evidence of anyone's emotional state, much less the imagined emotions of a literary character. However, you can examine Hamlet's actions and to see whether indirect evidence supports any reasons that might help you answer this question.

The reasoning for your main idea might look like this (with the reasons in chronological order):

Question: Does Hamlet truly love Ophelia?

Claim: Hamlet truly loves Ophelia.

Reason 1: Hamlet knowingly gives Ophelia painfully bad love poems.

Reason 2: Hamlet is deeply offended when Ophelia returns his love letters and poems.

Reason 3: Hamlet is deeply upset when Ophelia betrays him to her father and the King.

Reason 4: Hamlet swears that he will be as bold as Fortinbras.

Reason 5: Hamlet is emotionally overwhelmed when he learns of Ophelia's death.

Will these reasons offer a sound defense of your main idea? They might. One good sign is that all five of them are relevant reasons. They, like the main idea, are all ideas about Hamlet.

So far, so good.

But are they also credible reasons? And most importantly, are they logical? To determine these two qualities, you need to look more closely at the supporting evidence and underlying assumption for each reason. Here's the first one:

Claim: Hamlet truly loves Ophelia.

Reason 1: Hamlet knowingly gives Ophelia painfully bad love poems.

> Evidence: In 2.2, Polonius reads one of his poems to the King and Queen, showing us that 1) this is deeply felt love and 2) he's a painfully bad poet and admits it openly.

Assumption 1: True love is the only motive to knowingly give someone painfully bad love poems.

> Evidence: If you know you're a bad poet and send a love poem anyway, then you are motivated by love, not by the need to impress anyone or any other motive.

The first reason is credible because you have direct evidence from the scene noted that Hamlet wrote Ophelia this love poem. You also have the actual lines from the poem, and Polonius is right about them, too — they *are* bad. Hamlet himself admits that in the cover letter, which I can tell you from experience is a bad strategy.

To test the logic of the reason, you have to look at the assumption. It's appropriate for this situation because it's a general idea about the significance of painfully bad love poems. The assumption is also credible, although that might not be as clear to non-poets, because there's no reason for a poet to knowingly send someone a bad poem except as an uncontrollable expression of deep emotion. With a little extra explanation for non-poets, the assumption is also credible. So the first reason is both credible and logical.

Here's the next reason:

Claim: Hamlet truly loves Ophelia.

Reason 2: Hamlet is deeply offended when Ophelia returns his love letters and poems.

Evidence: In Act 3, Scene 1, Ophelia returns Hamlet's love letters and poems, and Hamlet is so shocked and offended that he tells her he never gave them to her.

Assumption 2: The return of love letters and poems is deeply offensive to someone who is truly in love.

This second reason looks less credible than the first one. You know that Hamlet says these words to Ophelia, but you don't know how he delivers the line. Is he hurt? Is he angry? Is he cool and untouched? You can't tell.

The underlying assumption is appropriate for this situation and appears to be credible. So you know that the reason is logical. However, without better evidence to defend this reason, the lack of credibility makes it a weak reason for the main idea.

Take a look at the third reason:

Claim: Hamlet truly loves Ophelia.

Reason 3: Hamlet is deeply upset when Ophelia betrays him to her father and the King.

Evidence: In Act 3, Scene 1, Hamlet figures out that Ophelia is being used against him by Polonius and the King. He then attacks Ophelia verbally and rants and raves about love and marriage.

Assumption 3: Betrayal by someone you truly love is deeply upsetting.

This reason is more credible than the second one because there's more evidence to validate it. After Hamlet asks a pointed question — "Where's your father?"— he goes off on Ophelia for the next several lines. He appears to be out of control with anger, and he broadens his attack on Ophelia to an attack on love and marriage in general. This is evidence of emotional distress, and it seems to be directly connected to his now-former girlfriend.

Is the assumption acceptable? It fits the situation, and if you've ever been betrayed by a loved one, you know how upsetting that can be. However, betrayal by *anyone* can be upsetting. It doesn't have to come from a loved one. So even though the credibility of the reason is okay, the logic isn't very solid, and that makes this a less effective reason in the argument.

Here's the fourth reason:

Claim: Hamlet truly loves Ophelia.

Reason 4: Hamlet swears that he would be as bold as Fortinbras.

Evidence: In Act 4, Scene 4, Hamlet encounters Fortinbras marching to attack Polish forces out of honor only. This makes him feel puny, so he swears he will be bold and deadly from now on.

Assumption 4: Swearing that you will be bold and deadly is evidence of true love.

This is a credible reason because the direct evidence for it is plain and sufficient. He does meet Fortinbras's army marching toward a pointless battle of honor. The sight makes him feel puny. He swears that henceforth his thoughts will "be bloody." Very good.

However, a credible reason is only good if it's also logical, and this reason is not logical because the underlying assumption is not a credible idea. Swearing to be bold and deadly is not evidence of true love. So no matter how well you can prove that Hamlet really swears this, the reason is useless because it's not logical.

Here is the last of your reasons:

Claim: Hamlet truly loves Ophelia.

Reason 5: Hamlet is emotionally overwhelmed when he learns of Ophelia's death.

Evidence: In Act 5, after Laertes jumps into Ophelia's grave to mourn her loudly, Hamlet steps out of hiding and challenges him, claiming that he loved Ophelia more than Laertes did.

Assumption 5: The death of someone you truly love is emotionally overwhelming.

The assumption is appropriate to this situation, and it's a credible idea, so you can conclude that this is a logical reason. There is also some direct evidence of Hamlet's grief over the death of Ophelia. He does jump into her grave with Laertes, and he claims to have forty thousand times more grief than Laertes — among other claims of greater emotion, such as beating Laertes in a crocodile-eating contest. If what Hamlet says about his grief is true, then this is solid evidence that Hamlet is overwhelmed by the news of Ophelia's death. That would make this a credible as well as logical reason.

However, this brings us back to the question itself. Is he telling the truth? Can you trust him? Is it just me, or does it seem strange that he's so competitive about who misses Ophelia most? He also seems to be overdoing it. Maybe he *is* a little crazy. A week earlier he was tormenting Ophelia at a little dinner theatre he put on, and now he misses her this much? The overdone display of grief suggests that he's more concerned with his rival Laertes than his dead former girlfriend. So while this reason is logical, it's not very credible.

In the same way that you have to adjust your main idea to fit the evidence of an inductive argument — never claiming more than what direct evidence actually defends — you also need to adjust your main idea to fit the reasons of a deductive argument. With convincing reasons, you can be bold. With weaker reasons, honesty requires you to be more restrained with your main idea.

In this case, after dumping the weak Fortinbras reason, you're left with four relevant, somewhat logical reasons to defend the claim that Hamlet loved Ophelia. I'll adjust those reasons so they better fit the actual evidence you have:

Reason 1: Hamlet knowingly gives Ophelia painfully bad love poems.

Reason 2: Hamlet seems to be offended when Ophelia returns his love letters and poems.

Reason 3: Hamlet is deeply upset when Ophelia betrays him to her father and the King.

Reason 4: Hamlet claims to be emotionally overwhelmed when he learns of Ophelia's death.

With reasons like these, what's the most honest answer to your question about Hamlet's alleged love for Ophelia? These reasons don't allow you to be as bold as Fortinbras with your answer. They don't *prove* that Hamlet loves Ophelia as much as he claims in Act 5. You have reason to believe he has true feelings for his former girlfriend because of the painfully bad love poems, but you have to take care in asserting just how much love is in Hamlet's heart by the time he jumps into the grave with Laertes. Whatever you decide, your answer should be presented as a possibility, not a sure thing.

AVOID BAD REASONS

With a deductive argument, reasons are bad when they lack relevance, credibility, or logic. That should come as no surprise. Sometimes a bad reason is an honest enough mistake, a seemingly sensible reason that, upon closer examination, is based on a flawed assumption or inadequate evidence. Sometimes a reason is bad because the relationship of claim and reason is based on some kind of emotional or symbolic association that defies any clear logical relationship. Sometimes a writer purposely builds a dishonest argument because there's no honest argument to be made. These are the ideas you really need to watch for. You don't want them in your own brain, and you certainly don't want to forward them along to others.

To wrap things up, here's a brief look at some common types of bad reasons. Writing professors refer to these as "logical fallacies," but you can also think of them as "screw-ups."

Begging the Question

With this screw-up, you don't offer any actual reasons for your claim. Instead, you defend your claim either by restating the claim with a rephrased version of the same idea or by offering no defense at all. Here's an example:

Claim: *Hamlet* is a confusing play.

Reason: It doesn't make any sense.

Because "confusing" and "doesn't make any sense" are roughly the same thing, the claim hasn't been defended by the reason. It's been restated. If you restate any idea enough, it will *look* like you're building a defense, but you're only repeating yourself. You're like one of those late-night radio commercials that repeat the phone number eighteen times in thirty seconds. The underlying assumption for this argument is "Confusing things don't make any sense," or "Confusing things are confusing." That's right, they are. Now offer me a reason *why* the play is confusing so that your essay will become less so.

A second way to beg the question — which is a strange phrase, isn't it? — is to present the claim and then move on to other ideas, such as how to implement your claim. You assume that your readers agree with you already and don't need to have the idea defended. Here's an example:

This country needs to stop recycling and stop it now. It may be popular and even fashionable to recycle your glass and plastic and paper products, but that doesn't make it a good practice. Likewise, there may be many reports in the media about overflowing landfills and polluted

> waters, but that too is not a good enough reason to recycle these products, and especially not now when so much is at stake.
>
> One of the most important things you should stop recycling is your newspaper....

And so on, from newspapers to plastic to glass to motor oil. The writer seems to have some reasons in mind for this unusual idea, but they never make it onto the page. Instead of explaining *why* to stop recycling, which is the more important question, the writer jumps ahead to the follow-up question of *how*. This is an engaging opening, but the essay will only work if you follow this provocative idea with a logical defense.

Post Hoc

This term is short for "post hoc, ergo propter hoc," which not only sounds cool but in Latin means "after this, therefore because of this." With this screw-up, you assume that if two events happen consecutively, the first event is the cause of the second event. Suppose, for example, that your girlfriend dumps you and two weeks later you notice substantial hair loss. You might from this observation draw the following deduction:

Claim: My girlfriend's departure caused substantial hair loss.

Reason: Her departure occurred shortly before my hair started falling out in clumps.

Assumption: Initial events are the cause of subsequent events. (After this, therefore because of this.)

It might be that — in this case, anyway — the first event *did* cause the second event. However, you're old enough to know that chronological order doesn't *guarantee* a causal relationship between two events. Sometimes things just happen in a certain order for no discernible reason. And if your social science electives teach you anything, it's that causal relationships are extremely difficult to establish. Because there's no evidence to support this underlying assumption, the assumption isn't credible and the reason that depends on it is not logical.

SLIPPERY SLOPE

This is the kind of screwed-up thinking that parents use to warn their children against misbehavior of any sort:

Claim: Don't eat that piece of candy.

Reason: It will rot your teeth out.

That's a pretty grim warning to give a four-year-old kid, but that's how it works when you're brought up on slippery-slope arguments. Don't even *think* about smoking cigarettes or you'll turn into a drug addict. Don't you steal money out of my change jar or you'll end up in prison. The only good thing about parental slippery-slope arguments is that they teach kids at an early age to stop listening to their parents.

The problem is the underlying assumption:

The first step in an undesirable direction will lead to extreme consequences in that same direction.

Yes, it sometimes happens that taking one step in a bad direction leads to extreme consequences in that same direction. However, there is no guarantee that one step in a bad direction will lead to dire consequences in that same direction. Life is not as simple as that. A lot of things can happen between A and Z.

As a human, you're able to learn from your mistakes. Other events or people might intervene, too. You might grow bored with misbehavior. Like a post hoc argument, then, the logic of a slippery slope argument is screwed up because the assumption is not a credible idea.

NON SEQUITUR

This is another cool Latin term that means "does not follow." While it might apply to any logical argument where the conclusion doesn't logically follow from its reasons or evidence, this term specifically applies to deductive arguments in which the claim and reason have *zero* logical connection. Post hoc and slippery-slope arguments have a slim but faulty connection. Non sequitur arguments are even more screwed up. Here's an example:

> Claim: The President mishandled the crisis in Central Asia.
>
> Reason: The President's approval ratings have dropped.
>
> Assumption: Presidential approval ratings are an appropriate measure for foreign policy crisis management.

With post hoc and slippery-slope arguments, the assumption might sometimes be true, but argument becomes screwed up because the assumption isn't always true. With non sequitur arguments, the assumption is *never* true. Because the assumption can never be credible, the reason will never be logical.

FALSE DILEMMA

This is sometimes called the "either/or" fallacy (or screw-up) because it claims that only two possible solutions exist. Either you must love your country as it is or you must leave it. Either you must support the troops or you're not a true patriot. Either you must call her tonight and apologize or you will regret it for the rest of your life.

The false dilemma is false because either the question is too simple — which is better, this or that? — or the underlying assumption is an idea that is almost never true — you have to pick one of these two choices. In both cases, the error is easy to see. First, you are almost never limited to just two options. Second, you don't have to make any choice at all. You can always wait to decide. Love it or leave it? I don't know. Let me think about that.

The practitioners of the false dilemma are often false as well — salespersons of ill repute and other knuckleheads who want to push you toward a particular conclusion by limiting the full range of actual options down to two. The first is a horrible option, such as self-exile. The second option isn't great, either, but it doesn't look so bad when compared to the horrible option.

You can fight off these false-dilemma knuckleheads by offering them alternatives to their two options. It will drive them *crazy*, and it will also protect you from this screwed-up kind of thinking.

BUT WAIT, THERE'S MORE

You could keep going all day with examples of screwed-up thinking.

It's true because it's a popular belief?

It's good because it's traditional?

It's not a problem because other people have problems?

It's true because someone who isn't really qualified says it's true?

I don't think so, says the careful student reader.

And the same goes for the careful student writer. As a writer, you can avoid screwed-up thinking by looking closely at your own reasons and making sure they are relevant, credible, and logical.

Chapter Ten

EARN YOUR CREDIBILITY

Your credibility as a writer is the confidence your readers place in you. It's their judgment of just how seriously they should take you and your ideas.

In this chapter, you'll take a closer look at this peculiar relationship you have with your readers. It's not the most rewarding relationship in the world. As you've seen already, it requires serious effort on your part. You have to be thorough in your research and thoughtful with your evidence. You have to plan and present your ideas carefully. And after all of that, your readers still might not take you seriously, possibly because of a stupid little mistake like using the word "defiantly" when you mean "definitely."

Credibility is tough to earn and easy to lose, but it helps if you know what your readers are looking for in a trustworthy writer. You can start by examining the nature of the writer-reader relationship. From there, you'll turn your attention to some practical tips for earning credibility from your readers.

THE KEY TO A SUCCESSFUL RELATIONSHIP IS YOU DOING ALL THE WORK

In recent months, I've learned a lot about readers from taking care of the cat that my former girlfriend forced on me when she moved out. "Here," she said, handing me the cat. "Evolve." I'm still not sure what she meant by that, nor have I been able to remember the cat's name, but I can tell you this — taking care of a cat teaches you *plenty* about the writer-reader relationship and credibility.

The first thing you learn is that your relationship with a cat exists solely for the benefit of the cat. Your job is to provide what the cat requires, and the cat's job is to grudgingly receive it. That's how it works with your readers, too. You provide. They receive. It's a one-way street.

More importantly, you are the only active participant in the owner-cat relationship. If you bring home the wrong brand of cat food, you have failed, and the cat can't do anything to fix your mistake. All she can do is walk away from the cat food she hates and maybe tear up the arm of the sofa to express her disappointment.

But even if you buy the right kind of cat food, your work isn't done. To be a credible provider, you also have to offer her the food in the right dish. If you put it in a dish she hates, you fail. *She* can't move it from the green bowl that she hates to the pink bowl that she loves. And she's certainly not going to change her mind about the green dish just because you put food in it. She's a cat, and she's made it perfectly clear that the green dish is out. If you don't want her to walk away and tear up your sofa, you have to put the food in the right dish.

It's the same story with your readers. The food is the essay you offer them. Your readers won't tear up your sofa if you offer them a shoddy idea, but they *will* walk away. They'll withdraw their confidence in you as a writer. But offering them a good idea is only the start. How you offer it also matters. They're your readers, and they've made it perfectly clear that they expect things to be just so. If you want to earn their confidence, you have to take their expectations seriously.

I'm starting to think that most writing professors are more like dogs than cats. Dogs will eat anything you give them and then thank you for it. They'll do everything they can to make you feel good about yourself, too, even if you don't deserve to. That's nice of them, I know, but you've probably figured out by now (inductively) that most of your actual readers are more like cats than dogs. Other professors, scholarship committees, court officials — these are people who are fussy not only about what you offer them but also how you offer it.

If you write a traffic judge a serious letter arguing that your fine should be reduced, for example, the judge isn't going to smile just to see an envelope with her name on it. She's not going to automatically reduce the fine and throw in a coupon for free pizza. That's how a dog would respond if a dog were a traffic judge, but a real traffic judge acts like a cat. You'll have to offer some good reasons to defend your idea, and you better not make your ideas unpalatable by explaining them with a handwritten note on unicorn stationery.

This is how it works with you and your readers. They are the cats, and their job is to sit in judgment while you do all the work. That's not fair to you. You would prefer a more equitable arrangement, and rightly so. However, if you want to be taken seriously, you have to do all the work. That starts by you accepting this lopsided relationship for what it is.

Do Credible Work

You earn your credibility by showing your readers the qualities that deserve to be taken more seriously — thoughtfulness, hard work, intelligence, precision, and so on. The main way you do this is by building a credible essay.

When you raise a good question, you show readers that you're an inquisitive thinker. When you gather and consider sufficient evidence for your question, you demonstrate that you're a hard worker. When you develop an insightful and convincing answer to your question, readers see how intelligent you are. When you translate your idea into a well-organized and technically excellent essay, you show readers that you are skilled. Your readers, impressed as they are by these qualities in your essay, are more likely to take you seriously.

In the same way, any weaknesses in your essay show readers that you lack important qualities as a writer, and you lose credibility. If you leave out evidence that readers know about, they'll wonder whether you've done that intentionally, to tilt the evidence in your favor, or from lack of effort. Either way, you'll have a harder time convincing them because you've lost some of their trust. If you offer a reason that isn't logical, your readers will find you less intelligent. That will throw all your ideas into question. If you're a worse speller than your readers, or if you include hilarious spell-checker errors, you might lose all credibility with your readers. That's like putting the cat food in the green dish. Your credibility might never recover from that kind of mistake.

Choose Your Words Carefully

Besides building a credible essay, you also earn — or more often risk losing — credibility by how you address your readers. My sister Nadine once told my mother to "get the hell out" of her bedroom. In the following weeks of retribution, it was discovered that Nadine had presented my mother with a reasonable suggestion. Nadine had been preening in front of the mirror in her underwear when Mom barged in to ask if she had the vacuum cleaner. Nadine, then in the bloom of her prolonged adolescence, was reasonable in making a claim for privacy. Her claim might have been taken seriously, too, if she had chosen her words more carefully.

Student writers, we hope, are not likely to swear at their readers, but that doesn't mean that they can't undo a lot of otherwise good work by choosing their words without care. Consider this paragraph:

Nowadays it sucks to be a student because there's never any way to make it happen without taking out TONS of student loans. My dad got GRANTS to go to school back in the day, free money, money he didn't even NEED, really, and his parents gave him money, too. Going to school now means basically taking out a mortgage on my LIFE. Is that fair? No way!

If we look just at the observation and its short bit of evidence, this is a reasonable opinion that has some basis in reality. For this student, going to school requires many dollars in student loans. Compared to the public support that was available to the student's father, the student is in a far worse situation. However, that's not what you notice about this paragraph. You notice the CAPITAL LETTERS and conversational tone and the word "sucks." This approach is not uncommon for student writers. Wanting to connect with readers, they work hard to *not* show off their intelligence with smarty-pants techniques such as precise language and grammatical sentences. Instead, they translate their complex ideas into a friendly but vague conversational style.

Foolish student writers! That's not how you earn credibility. Your readers don't want to be your friend. They are cats, and cats are critical, and if you're going to connect with cats, you do so by rising to their high standards and earning their trust. That means addressing your readers precisely, intelligently, and respectfully. If you have a good idea — and I'm confident you do — then translate that idea into exact, formal language and assume that your reader is up to the task of understanding it. Don't try to be friends with your catlike readers. That only makes them reject you — and probably your idea, too.

Besides adopting a more serious tone, you should also avoid inflammatory words. Swear words, for example, are almost never credible in the college essay. Vulgarity rarely works. You know that, though. A more common mistake is to present your ideas with words that make fun of topics or ideas that are important to your readers. In doing that, you make fun of your readers, too.

Consider these three topic sentences for the same paragraph:

Senate Bill 211 could have the unintended consequence of raising the mortality rate in our state.

Senate Bill 211 is a threat to children.

Senate Bill 211 is ridiculous.

Now imagine that you support Senate Bill 211.

In the first topic sentence, the writer states an idea that you can see you should take seriously, and there's nothing here to put you on the defensive. This is only a *possibility* to consider. The writer assumes that it would be an unintended consequence, not a malicious act by its sponsors. The sentence is objective about its concern. As a supporter, this sentence is still challenging for you. You may not want to hear this. However, because the writer brings it up respectfully and objectively, you are likely to read the paragraph that follows with an open mind. The writer has earned enough credibility for that.

The second topic sentence is less precise, so you're not sure what to expect from the paragraph, but the real barrier is the word "threat." Senate Bill 211 might indeed be a threat, so the idea might be accurate, but that word suggests intentional harm, and that could make you feel defensive about the bill, even though you don't know yet what the writer means by this word. The vagueness gives the impression that the whole bill is a threat, too, so that's more reason to continue with a much less open mind. The writer has made the job of convincing you more difficult by using this inflammatory word. It lowers your confidence in the objectivity of the writer.

The third topic sentence is insulting, and you as a supporter know that the real-world evidence about this bill doesn't support that kind of disrespect. The bill isn't worthy of ridicule. It's thoughtful work. It might not be perfect, but it wasn't written by baboons. When you see a vague and insulting topic sentence like that, it almost doesn't matter what follows. The writer has shown contempt for something you support, and that's contempt you might easily feel on a personal level. If you were a cat, this is when you would tear up the sofa. As a human, if you read the paragraph at all, you will read it with distrust for this writer. A single word has cost the writer most of his or her credibility.

If you've taken the time to build a good essay, take a little more time to choose your words carefully. Presenting your argument with careful, appropriate, respectful language helps to preserve the credibility you've earned.

RESPECT THE VIEWS OF OTHERS

You also earn credibility by showing respect for those with whom you disagree. And by "showing respect," I don't mean faking it. It's easy enough to say that you respect the views of others, but to actually show that respect, you need to state their positions fairly, adapt your own position in light of their ideas, and rebut their positions honestly. If a person you disagree with happens to be one of your readers, this kind of treatment helps them to take you and your ideas seriously. However, even if a reader agrees with your views, you earn additional credibility by providing consideration of other evidence and ideas.

One worry that student writers often have about addressing alternative claims or contradictory evidence is that it will weaken their arguments. You should only worry about that when your argument is weak. If, for example, your argument makes sense only if you ignore contradictory evidence, then presenting all the evidence will make that flaw clear to readers. Or if you present an idea as the best answer to a question but it's really just one of three equally good answers, then presenting those other two equally good answers will make readers wonder what makes your chosen answer any better than the others. The solution to this problem, however, is not to hide the evidence that makes your argument look weak. Your argument doesn't just look weak. It *is* weak. The solution is to write a better argument.

I've also heard student writers quietly confess that they

don't want to appear wimpy by having to qualify their ideas or acknowledge that other alternatives are also pretty good. I assume that this is a lingering bit of persuasive paper strategy, the urge to bowl the readers over with boldness.

The goal of the college essay is not to share strong opinions. The goal is to share honest opinions. Considering and respecting alternate views helps you to improve your own ideas, to make them more honest, by tempering them and expanding the basis of evidence for your judgments. A bold display of unearned confidence is thus a sign of weakness, not strength. You're overcompensating for something, the careful reader thinks — which is a catty thing for readers to think, but then again, your readers *are* catlike.

The best way to show respect for alternative positions is to present them fairly and accurately. It might be tempting to present them negatively or to present a weakened version of any opposing arguments. However, an informed reader will see what you're doing and hold it against you. If the opposing position really is weaker, you should be polite and honest about that and let readers see that weakness for themselves. There's no need to beat up on the opposition.

Suppose you have just written a convincing argument that people should stop drinking cow milk because 80 percent of cow milk now comes from mega-dairies that pollute the environment with methane and liquid manure. One opposing position is that children should drink cow milk because it's such an efficient way for their developing bodies to get the nutrients they need. Another opposing position is that people should drink only organic milk because it doesn't contain any of the drugs used to make cows produce large quantities of milk. How do you include those views in your essay? Here's one option:

> It will come as no surprise that some people have no real concern for the environment. All they care about is meeting their own needs. Parents, for example, might say that cow milk is an essential food for growing children. That might be true, but a lot of good it will do those kids if they don't have an environment to grow up in.
>
> Your local hippie farmers may *look* like they care about the environment because so much of the environment is caked to their boots and overalls. They may claim, too, that their organic milk is safer because they don't pump their cows full of pregnancy hormones. But the fact is that whether these farmers look eco-friendly or not, and whether the milk is safe or not, the hippie cows still produce the same amount of manure and methane as mega-dairy cows. The milk might be better to drink, but the cows are still bad for the environment.
>
> There are reasons to say yes to cow milk as food, but that's not the real issue here. The real issue is saving the environment. Without a safe environment, we die. Every time these parents and hippie farmers say yes to cow milk, they're saying no to Mother Earth. They're committing a slow, lactose-friendly form of suicide.

These are bold words, anti-bovine student writer, and while I salute your passion, this presentation of alternative positions makes me question your objectivity. By asserting that parents and "hippie farmers" don't really care about the environment, you've demonstrated that you either don't understand them or that you think that people don't *really* care about the environment unless they care in the same way and to the same degree that you care. Either way, that's small-minded thinking. Your credibility has decreased.

You've also dismissed these views quickly and entirely. Isn't a parent's concern for nutrition worthy of consideration? Doesn't organic farming, at least to some degree, address the problems of mega-dairies? To be fair and accurate, you should present those views in more detail and without bashing them at the same time. See what you think of this:

> It's understandable that parents in particular would object to abolishing cow milk because they have come to rely on it for their children's health. Cow milk provides easily assimilated calcium to help developing bones, and it's loaded with other vitamins that children in particular need. Removing cow milk from a child's diet would require parents to find alternative methods for supplying these nutrients, and that might not always be convenient.
>
> However, it's still important to consider the long-term perspective with this issue. A child's health and development are very important, but equally important is the health of the planet. To improve the health of the planet, we have to at least reduce our dependence on cow milk so we can reduce the number of cows. If parents can't safely replace cow milk, then they shouldn't. However, they can stop drinking it themselves, and if they can find ways to reduce or remove cow milk from their children's diet, they should. Every little bit helps.

Presenting ideas accurately takes more time, and so does responding to those ideas thoughtfully. The organic farmers will thus require a better paragraph of their own, a paragraph that you'll have to write when you have a little more time. In the paragraphs above, however, you can see the difference it makes to more honestly present the specific benefits of cow milk, the reason that parents might have for using it, and the challenges parents might face if they *didn't* use it. The language is more neutral and free of disparagement. You even have a quiet show of empathy for these hard-working parents, along with shared concern for the health of the children. Children are our future, after all.

What's even better, however, is how you now respond to this more accurate and objective parental position. That response illustrates the other two ways that you take opposing views seriously — with concessions and honest rebuttals. In the original version, you conceded nothing to the parental position. If anything, the possible objection of parents made you bolder in your attack. You called parents environment-haters, and said their use of milk was a slow form of suicide. That was bold and colorful, but it was also too much.

In this version, you wisely offer a concession in response to a parental objection. If a parent can't safely remove cow milk from a child's diet, then they shouldn't. Your main idea remains largely in place — stop drinking milk to remove the need for and damage caused by mega-dairies — but this concession to certain circumstances is sensible and makes the idea more complex and more palatable to parents. It's more realistic to ask your readers to reduce their use of cow milk than it is to ask them to eliminate it. This isn't a gimmick on your part, either. The concession is warranted. You saw that and made your idea better with this concession. That increases your credibility.

The second part of this improved response is your rebuttal to the parental objection. Instead of going after parents with attack language, you now respectfully put their concern for children next to your concern for the planet. No name-calling is required. Careful readers can see that it's not reasonable to dismiss long-term problems for the sake of short-term convenience. When you let the evidence make your point for you, and when you concede parts of your point as required by their objections, your readers are much more likely to keep thinking about this.

Keep this in mind when you respond to the organic farmers. They might not be as hard on the earth as the mega-dairies. Maybe you can offer them a concession, too. Maybe they and the parents can get together to provide kids with healthier milk from environmentally healthier dairies. If so, your idea will be even wiser and you will be even more credible.

You can't always offer reasonable concessions to objections. Some objections are simply wrong. When that's the case, you have to respond firmly and take even more care to explain objectively and respectfully why an objection is wrong. In those cases, remember that the fault is with the idea, not with those who hold that idea. Your goal should not be to shame those readers away from that bad idea but to help them understand its flaws and why your position makes more sense. You need to be neighborly about it. You need to be respectful.

In return, your readers will find you more credible and take your ideas more seriously. You're still doing all the work in this relationship, but at least you have that small measure of respect. That's something.

KNOW YOUR READERS

To show the proper respect for your readers, you also have to know your readers. You have to pay attention to them and understand them as well as the moment allows. You have to put yourself in their position, looking back at you and your questionable credibility. This is one more lesson that a cat is willing to teach you about your readers.

To get my former girlfriend's cat to stop clawing the furniture, I worked diligently to understand her perspective. I studied how she responded to different foods, different bowls, and different television programs. I probably spent a hundred dollars on DVDs of birds and squirrels and mice until I found the turtle DVD that keeps her calm while I'm at work. It's taken time and discipline to figure out how she looks at the situation, but I get it now. By getting into her head, I can do my job for her a lot more effectively. And not only that, but I have earned, I believe, her respect. That's a strange thing to be proud of, I know, but I'll take it.

For you and your college essay, it won't be quite as hard to figure out how to look at yourself from the reader's perspective. You are writing the essay because it was assigned. So read the assignment instructions carefully. You'll find that they are full of clues about what your reader expects from you. Hint: Your reader expects an essay that follows those instructions.

Your professor also expects you to give the essay serious thought and serious work. It wasn't assigned so that you could knock it off in an hour and go play video games. It wasn't assigned so that your roommate could do it for you. The essay is there as your opportunity to learn something new. So go learn something new. Your professor can't do that for you. Neither can your roommate.

If you're writing to a general audience for some other purpose, take even more time to consider who your readers are and what they expect from you. Is this a letter to the editor? If so, follow the guidelines. If they say the letter should be no more than 200 words long, don't assume they'll be twice as happy with 400 words.

And while you're at it, consider how other newspaper readers might answer the question that your letter answers. Try to be respectful of their views. What issues will they have with your answer? What are the words that will trigger anger or defensiveness from them? Choose your words carefully. That will be easier if you try to understand the reasons they have for their ideas. That makes you a more credible writer because it makes you more respectful and honest.

In the end, all this hard work to build credibility might not be enough to win your readers' approval. That's okay. That's their option. They are cats, after all, and cats will not be told what to do. Even so, your job as a writer is to work on their behalf as honestly and respectfully as you can so that nothing in how you present your idea will prevent your readers from accepting that idea on its own merits. The more you do that, the less likely they are to walk away.

Chapter Eleven

MAKE BETTER ARGUMENTS

So far, you've been introduced to the basic process of building an argument and presenting your argument in a good but probably not great college essay. Learning how to do this on your own is no small accomplishment, so congratulations, less foolish student writer.

But make no mistake — this is just an introduction. The book has purposely avoided the technical terminology and rhetorical theories that you find in most argument books. You've only tiptoed through the basics of formal logic. That isn't because these things *should* be avoided. It's just easier to build a working understanding of how to do argument with a simpler model.

You can do better than that, however, and in this chapter, you'll get a glimpse of a brighter future by looking at the three popular and more complex models for written arguments — the classical, Toulmin, and Rogerian approaches to argument. Each offers a variation of what you've learned so far but takes you into greater complexities of thought and presentation.

THE CLASSICAL ARGUMENT

Argument has been a branch of learning for thousands of years. When you talk about classical argument, you're referring to a broad band of theories and strategies dating back to the ancient Greeks and Romans. This includes ideas about how logic works and how different elements of argument — writer, reasons, audience — join together to make an argument more or less effective. This also includes theories about how to effectively present your ideas to others. We don't have time or paper to explain it all here, but you should at least be aware of two important classical concepts — the rhetorical triangle and the classical presentation.

THE RHETORICAL TRIANGLE

The rhetorical triangle does *not* refer to the summer when Aristotle and Socrates dated the same young Athenian woman. That may be how the Greek tabloids employed the term back in the day, but for you it points to the three main elements of what's also known as "the rhetorical situation": logos, ethos, and pathos.

Logos means "word," and in this context it refers to the written or spoken argument and the internal qualities of that argument. Are the reasons logical? Is the evidence sufficient? Is this the best possible answer that the current evidence supports? Arguments that defend an idea by emphasizing reasons and evidence are said to make logical appeals.

Aristotle said that these were the strongest types of arguments, and nobody argues with Aristotle, including most writing professors. I certainly don't. That's why this book spends so much time looking at evidence and how evidence connects to your main idea, either directly or indirectly through reasons.

Ethos means "character," as in the quality of your character as a writer and showing an audience why you deserve their confidence. It focuses on the writer or speaker, the originator of the argument, and on establishing the degree to which this writer is trustworthy. The word I've used for ethos is "credibility." Especially in the last chapter, you can see that credibility is built by how you behave as a writer. This includes how thoroughly you consider evidence and how open-minded you are about your question. It includes how well you handle that evidence with care. It includes the words you choose and your attitude toward your readers.

In rare cases — such as court cases, for example — you might build an argument that focuses on your character as its central strength. If you can show a judge that you're not the sort of person who would steal a NASCAR poster from Walmart, then even without a clear logical argument, you might win the case with an ethical appeal. In most arguments, however, ethos is not the central focus but an important supporting element. The more credible you are, the more others are willing to consider the logic of your argument.

Pathos means "suffering" or "experience." It focuses on the audience of the argument. While pathos often refers to the emotions of the audience — including suffering — it also includes other built-in elements of your audience such as beliefs, values, moral guidelines, and so on. Most importantly, it refers to your audience's capacity to imagine and empathize with the situation at hand.

Arguments that work to stir up the emotions, sympathies, and memories of readers are called emotional appeals or appeals to pathos. You see them all the time in advertising. Political ads often attempt to stir up fear or anger in their audience and then connect those feelings to an opposing candidate. All those erectile dysfunction ads like to show happy couples taking quiet walks together or just *shopping* with that particular gleam in their eyes. That's not a logical appeal. Those ads are stirring something else up in the audience, let me tell you.

Pathos is often used by knuckleheads to get what they want by wooing your heart and imagination instead of discussing the matter with your mind. That use of pathos is often effective, so you have to be on your guard against it all the time. However, even in an honest, logical argument, it's still important to connect with your readers, to show them how your argument works in their personal corner of reality. To do that, you might offer stories, hypothetical situations, case studies, and so on to make your ideas something they can imagine for themselves and apply to their own lives. That's pathos, too, and when used honestly in this way, it makes an ethical or logical argument even more effective.

THE CLASSICAL PRESENTATION

Aristotle said that an argument needed only two parts — the proposition or claim, which you present first, and then your defense of that proposition. He allowed for the addition of an introduction or conclusion or both, if the situation called for it, but otherwise, he thought arguments needed to remain simple and flexible.

The Romans — most notably Cicero — couldn't resist fiddling with these Greek ideas and arrived at a slightly more complicated model than Aristotle's two- to four-part argument. Their model for presentation — which remains popular and effective to this day — includes six or seven elements, depending on whom you talk to. I'll group those within the three parts of the essay that we've used:

The opening can be one to several paragraphs long, depending on the situation. In some situations, you might only use one or two of these techniques listed below. In other cases, such as with a scientific paper, you might spend several paragraphs laying out the background information before getting started. Here are the optional components, and to put you in the right mood, we'll use the old-school Latin terms.

Exordium gets the audience's attention in some way. It engages their interest or sympathies. An appeal to pathos is not a bad idea at this point.

Narratio explains the situation. It provides background information about the question at issue and what's led up to this disagreement. It might also show readers why this matters for them and others.

Propositio is the presentation of the main idea of the argument — your claim or thesis. This typically comes at or near the end of the introduction.

Partitio is the presentation of how the argument is arranged or divided. It identifies the major parts of the argument so that the audience knows generally what to expect. Although this is particularly helpful with speeches, you should also use it with longer written arguments. It's part of guiding your readers.

Here's an example of an opening that uses all four classical elements:

> [*Exordium*:] In a recent *People* magazine poll, 59 percent of the respondents said that they hated to write. On a recent reality television show, only one of six contestants was willing to sit at a table and take a college-level essay exam, even when offered a hundred dollars. [*Narratio*:] What's the problem? People have become uncomfortable with the written word. They've come to prefer talking to others and using key hand gestures. But that seems to be changing because of cell phones. Young people today would rather text someone than have to listen to their lame conversation, so the use of writing is suddenly on the rise. The problem now is how best to use cell phones to train this next generation of writers. [*Propositio*:] This essay offers a great solution — a new cell phone designed by English teachers that requires correct spelling and punctuation for all text messages. [*Partitio*:] We'll look first at the cell phone's features and then at how this device has already improved the writing skills of dozens of children of English teachers.

The body of the essay does most of the work of any argument, and that's the case with the classical model as well. The body contains the two most important elements.

Confirmatio is the presentation of your main idea about the question under consideration. More importantly, it is the defense of that main idea with reasons and evidence. In the classical model, you often arrange these defenses from weakest to strongest or from most obvious to most subtle. Each reason is supported by an underlying assumption that you assume the audience already accepts. This section is typically the majority of the essay. Most of this book has focused on how to build a good confirmatio. It just does so without using any Latin.

Confutatio is your preemptive response to other positions. This starts with a fair and accurate summary of those views and then consideration of the weaknesses in those views. Depending on those weaknesses, you might respectfully refute those views fully or concede some stronger aspects.

The closing: In the classical model, the **peroratio** brings the essay to a close. It summarizes the entire argument and explains to readers why your idea is the strongest available answer to the question at issue. It also tries to leave a strong impression with readers.

You saw good peroratio with the two examples of closing in Chapter Eight. The second-half-of-an-anecdote closing spent a lot of time summarizing its evidence. The call-to-action closing showed readers how to apply this idea to their own lives by, of course, calling them to action. A third option would be to put your idea into a broader context in order to underscore its importance to readers.

THE TOULMIN ARGUMENT

In his 1958 book, *The Uses of Argument*, philosopher Stephen Toulmin proposed that arguments based on formal logic, which had been the norm since Aristotle, didn't adequately describe how argument works in real life. He adapted and expanded the terms of the deductive argument to create a model that he believed more closely reflected how people actually argue. This model is particularly helpful in analyzing the arguments of others, but you can also use it to build and test your own argument.

CLAIM, GROUNDS, AND WARRANTS

The three central terms in the Toulmin model are claim, grounds, and warrants. These are similar in meaning to the claim, reason, and assumption used in deductive reasoning, but there are some important differences:

Claims: As with the classical argument, the claim is your conclusion, the main idea that your argument asserts and defends. The claim will be a reasonable opinion of your own:

You should accept his apology.

Grounds: This is your defense of your opinion, the majority of your essay. It's a collective term that can mean direct evidence or reasons — that are themselves supported by more grounds — or both evidence and reasons together. The emphasis, however, is on the real world, not simply on the logical consistency of deduction. So even if you use reasons, you need to keep them grounded in the real world with whatever evidence they require.

Here's one reason for the claim:

He didn't realize he was being such a jerk.

Warrants: On first glance, this term appears to work like the underlying assumption from deductive reasoning, but with Toulmin, the relationship is not as mathematically clear as with formal logic. This is an important advantage of the Toulmin model. Rather than looking at just one generalization — the deductive assumption — to guarantee the logical relationship of the claim and grounds, the Toulmin model looks for a more general understanding of what ideas need to be "givens" in order for readers to accept that the grounds are a sufficient defense of the claim. This is where Toulmin moves furthest from formal logic and closest to reality. So pay attention.

In formal logic, the assumption for the argument above would be a generalization like this: "You should accept the apologies of people who didn't realize, at the time, that they were behaving badly." If you accept that idea, you have a logical argument. However, it may not be a convincing argument because the assumption is an odd idea, not a particularly strong value that you can count on readers accepting. In the Toulmin model, you note all the underlying ideas that are required for the grounds to be a sufficient defense of the claim:

It benefits you to forgive others, whether or not they ask for forgiveness.

Accepting apologies helps to rebuild broken relationships.

It's good to rebuild broken relationships.

People unaware of their bad behavior are more forgivable than others.

Forgiveness has meaningful impact on lives and relationships.

If you accept these warrants — and perhaps others, depending on your and your readers' views of the world — then the claim and grounds become an effective argument. If you see any problems with one or more of these ideas, then the logic of the argument starts to break down.

This is closer to how real-life reasoning works. Few people stop to chart out the formal logic of their beliefs. However, that doesn't stop anyone from drawing conclusions. You look at evidence and ideas, and you then use them to form new opinions of our own. Your underlying assumptions, however, remain veiled and complicated. It's more like an underlying web of ideas than a set of separate assumptions. The Toulmin model is thus a good way to think about what the underlying web of ideas looks like and then use this more complex understanding to analyze and develop arguments. That's why we call these *warrants* rather than just *the* warrant. They are legion.

BACKING, QUALIFIERS, AND REBUTTALS

Three other terms come into play as important supporting concepts. These help to bring your argument even closer to the reality of complex issues and the tangled web of human thinking: backing, qualifiers, and rebuttals.

Backing is any defense you provide for any of the warrants. Suppose, for example, that when you look at your warrants, you find that one of them is questionable. If you provide support for that weak warrant, it's called backing rather than grounds. You might back it up with direct evidence. You might back it up with reasons and indirect evidence. In the list of warrants above, one idea in particular looks weak:

It benefits you to forgive others, whether or not they ask for forgiveness.

This is an idea that you need in order to convince your audience to forgive him, whoever he is, but it's an idea that isn't immediately convincing. If you explain, however, why this benefits the reader ethically and materially, and if your ideas and evidence are convincing, then you have successful backing for that warrant and your claim becomes that much stronger.

Qualifiers are adjustments to your claim that you make in light of conflicting evidence or specific situations or alternative positions. They limit the scope of the claim so that it doesn't include objectionable applications. These are concessions you make to potential objections.

Suppose, for example, that you anticipate the objection that accepting an apology from an abusive guy might give him permission to continue being abusive. That's a reasonable objection, and you agree that in cases of abuse, an apology might not be sufficient grounds for forgiveness. It's certainly not your intent to let a dangerous person continue to be dangerous. The person you have in mind was insensitive and possibly more humorless than he realized for long stretches of time. He didn't actually harm anyone, but he wasn't much fun, either. That's what you mean by "jerk." You can respond to those potential objections, then, by limiting the boundaries of your claim with a qualifier that excludes abusive behavior:

> Unless he has been abusive, you should accept his apology.

In addition to limiting the application of your claim, qualifiers might also include words like "sometimes" or "often" to limit the frequency or reliability of your idea.

If you can think of other situations that limit the application of this idea, or even if you imagine that there *might* be situations that limit the application of this claim, then you can pop a "probably" into the claim to acknowledge that weakness:

> Unless he has been abusive, you should probably accept his apology.

Qualifiers help you to better define your claim and be more honest about how well your evidence and reasons actually defend that idea. The sad fact is that real-world arguments almost never prove anything conclusively, so you need qualifiers if you're going to make realistic claims.

Rebuttals in the Toulmin model are not rebuttals of opposing positions but the opposing positions themselves. They are the anticipated counterarguments to your claim, grounds, or warrants. You include them in your argument to show the limitations or possible exceptions to your argument. They help you to be more honest about your claim and also to be more comprehensive about all of the evidence and objections out there.

Rebuttals can be compelling and cause you to add qualifiers to your claim. Adding a huge "unless" to your entire claim might, as in the case of abusive apologizers, make the entire claim invalid in certain situations. Sometimes, however, a rebuttal is not supported by a sufficient defense of its own and thus should be addressed and defused with more grounds or backing. The key, once again, is to be realistic. Including rebuttals does not weaken your argument. It makes it more honest and complex, more realistic, and that's the goal with the Toulmin model.

THE ROGERIAN ARGUMENT

If you're old enough, you might remember Fred Rogers, the creator and host of public television's *Mr. Rogers' Neighborhood*. In this long-running children's show, Mr. Rogers spoke directly into the camera and asked his young viewers, "Won't you be my neighbor?" The Rogerian argument takes Mr. Rogers' neighborliness a step further. It assumes that instead of timid four-year-olds, you face a more intelligent and hostile audience, people who disagree with your ideas and have strong opinions of their own. The Rogerian model takes that audience seriously but still asks them, in spite of their hostility, "Won't you be my neighbor?"

The Mr. Rogers of the Rogerian argument is not Fred but Carl Rogers, a psychologist and therapist. In their 1970 book, *Rhetoric: Discovery and Change*, Young, Becker, and Pike first presented his ideas to the rhetoric crowd. The Rogerian model begins and ends with respect for your audience. You must take care to understand the audience, state all ideas with neutral language, be fair and accurate in presenting the views of others, and be honest in assessing and acknowledging the strengths of those views. When presenting your own views, you must do so neutrally, accurately, and honestly — and you should add qualifiers to your claims as required by the merits of the audience's views.

The Rogerian argument looks for common interests and beliefs between you and your audience and ways by which the audience can benefit from shifting their position toward your position. Ideally, however, the argument brings both views together in a way that allows them to complement each other. When it comes to presentation, many variations have been proposed, but it's common to organize a Rogerian essay by moving through these five stages:

STAGE 1: PRESENT THE ISSUE AND YOUR INVITATION

In the Rogerian approach, the goal is not to win an argument. The goal is to build agreement — as much as possible — between opponents. The opening of the Rogerian essay, then, begins this process by presenting the issue over which you and your opponents disagree and acknowledging that within this issue, there is room for reasonable disagreement. However, you also propose to your readers that through a respectful exchange of ideas, it's possible for you and your opponents to find some common ground upon which you can agree.

STAGE 2: PRESENT YOUR OPPONENTS' POSITION

The next step toward agreement is to present the views of your opponents fairly and accurately and without any judgment so that they know that they've been heard and respected. This requires you to first shut up and listen to those views — figuratively or literally — and then show them some respect. This also requires a willingness on your part to change your own mind if your opponents have better ideas. You have to be willing to adapt your views as their evidence or reasons require.

STAGE 3: PRESENT CONTEXTS IN WHICH YOUR OPPONENTS' POSITION IS VALID

Even after you've been open-minded about the merits of your opponents' views, and even after you've taken the time to truly understand the thinking of your opponents, you won't be writing this argument unless you still believe that your ideas make more sense generally. However, you've probably discovered that, at least in some situations, your opponents' views are valid. In that case, give your opponents credit.

By honestly acknowledging the limited validity of the opposing argument, you help to calm any defensiveness in your audience because you are clearly *not* saying their ideas are entirely bad. Second, you build your own credibility as a more honest and precise writer. Third, this provides some common ground. Your opponents might believe their position is valid in broader contexts than this, but at least you and they agree on this particular point. That's a step in the right Rogerian direction. It can help your opponents to more seriously consider aspects of your position.

STAGE 4: PRESENT YOUR POSITION AND THE CONTEXTS IN WHICH IT IS VALID

As with other arguments, you still spend the larger part of your essay presenting your own position. However, in the Rogerian argument, you only do this after you have shown respect to your audience and their opposing views. It's important that you put the audience first and yourself second. You've considered their ideas openly and honestly. Now it's their turn to consider yours. The time you've invested in your audience makes them far more likely to invest some time in you.

As you explain your main idea and present the evidence and reasons that defend it, you must again be honest and accurate. Let the evidence speak for itself. Guard against smugness. Wherever you see common ground between your position and theirs, be a good neighbor about it and point that out. After you've done this, you should also discuss the limitations of your position. It's only fair. And here again is an opportunity to establish common ground.

STAGE 5: SHOW HOW YOUR OPPONENTS' POSITION BENEFITS FROM ADOPTING ELEMENTS OF YOURS

The goal of traditional argument is to present what you believe is the best answer to a question and prove to readers that they need to get their heads out of their shorts and accept your idea. The closing of a traditional argumentative essay thus ends appropriately with your main idea and a summary of the weighty defense you have made. The goal of the Rogerian argument, on the other hand, is to find agreement with others, so the closing of the Rogerian essay works a bit differently. It looks for ways to build a more neighborly understanding.

The closing does not expect your opponents to abandon their ideas and adopt yours. The closing lets the opponents keep their ideas but encourages them, based on the common ground you've established, to at least adopt elements of your position and integrate these into their own position — to strengthen their position by incorporating elements of your position. This might also include asking them to accept limitations or qualifications to their position.

You can see how this works in real-world conflicts. If you and your employer can't agree about whether your employer should pay for your health insurance, a Rogerian argument might end by showing how the benefits your employer would receive from a healthier you outweigh the cost of insurance premiums. And if that's still too much money for your employer to accept, you could also explain how catastrophic health insurance, which costs far less than comprehensive insurance, would still benefit you and your employer. On that point, at least, you might both agree.

The Rogerian argument, as a complete model, will be difficult for you to apply in your work as a student writer because it doesn't really fit the rhetorical situation of student, professor, and essay. You're not usually in a position to change your professor's mind because you're still new to the neighborhood and your professor has been here for a while. However, you can always take this attitude of respect and put it to good use in any argument. You can also make good use of a Rogerian approach when you consider evidence and try to find your own best answer. It will help you to be more open to possibilities you haven't considered.

The Rogerian model works best in real-life situations, such as after you've been a knucklehead and have turned loved ones into former loved ones, or when conflicts naturally arise within any community to which you belong. When conflicts emerge, respect for others is often the first thing to go, and that only makes the conflict worse. A Rogerian approach restores respect first, and that helps you and your loved ones or neighbors move back toward resumption of your functional — if not always harmonious — relationships.

Chapter Twelve

THE HUMBLE ARGUMENT

One thing to remember about writing the college essay is that this is intended to be a process more than a product. It's true that the product is what earns the grade, but trust me, your professors don't assign these essays so they'll have more to read after everyone else has gone to bed. They assign essays so that you'll learn something by going through the process of writing one. They want you to learn how to think for yourself within their disciplines.

Do you have to write a psychology paper? Good! Maybe now, your professor thinks, you'll start to *think* like a psychologist instead of just regurgitating psychological terminology on midterm exams. Do you have to write an environmental science paper? Good! Maybe now you'll start to look at the environment like a scientist instead of just memorizing a lot of lousy facts. Do you have to write a philosophy paper, a history paper, an economics paper? Good! This is your chance to borrow your professor's academic discipline and take it for a drive around the block. This is a gift!

THE HUMBLE ESSAY AS A PROCESS

How do you accept this gift from your professors? You do so very simply, by adopting with humility and confidence the process you've learned in this book:

1. *Find a good question.* It should be one that engages your curiosity and is appropriate for the assignment. It should be debatable, so that you're forced to figure out your own opinion about the answer. It should be researchable, so that your answer will be based upon direct or indirect evidence from the real world.

2. *Gather and consider relevant evidence.* Rather than looking for evidence to defend a pre-existing opinion, look for evidence that's relevant to your question. Use that evidence to test old ideas and look for new ones.

3. *Decide on the best answer.* Use your evidence to reasonably decide which answer makes the most sense. Don't claim more than the evidence allows, but don't back away from taking a stand, either. Remember that the best answer is not the boldest but the most honest.

4. *Present your argument to others.* Plan your essay before you write it. Draft it carefully, offering good evidence and reasons and giving credit where credit is due. Guide your readers through the essay with an effective opening, clear topic sentences and transitions throughout

the body, and an effective closing. Proofread closely so that you remove any distractions.

It may be fruitless for me to tell you that education and grades have little in common. You've been trained for too long to care about grades, and you haven't graduated yet, so you have no way of knowing how badly you've been duped. Even so, grade-hungry student writers, when you focus on this process rather than just creating an attractive product, you gain what your professors want most for you to gain — understanding — and this happens regardless of the grade you get for the finished product. But you're also more likely to get, as a parting gift, a decent grade for the product, too.

That being said, I understand that most college students are not interested in the writing process. They have learned over the years to be product-oriented, so when I tell them about the importance of this process, they agree that the writing process is great and everything, but what they really want to know is what I'm looking for on the next essay.

I'll tell you what I'm looking for, I tell them. I'm looking for you to find a good question for this topic. Then I'm looking for you to gather and consider as much relevant evidence as time allows. Then think about it. Don't be a knucklehead. Take some time, and then decide on the best answer that the evidence gives you.

No, they say, not that. We know that. Writing is a process, and that's super important. But what should the *paper* look like?

It should look like your main idea, I tell them.

They wait for more.

Start with your idea, I say, the answer to your question. Then list the evidence and reasons that led you to decide on that answer as the best one currently available. Then organize that list. Look for internal patterns that you might use because they seem to be most effective. However, if you think an external pattern makes more sense — say least-to-most important reasons — go with that. After you've drafted the body of the essay, develop an effective opening and closing. Remember when we talked about that? And then make sure the body of the essay guides your readers carefully.

No, they say, speaking slowly now so that I will understand them. Not that. What should the paper *look* like?

Always, they come back to me with their questions about the product. Always, I fight them off with answers about the process of writing and the more difficult idea that the essay should be shaped like your answer and the evidence behind it. Yes, they tell me. We understand. Thank you. That's a really great idea for us to keep in mind. But what are you *looking* for?

Trying to be more positive in my outlook generally, I shared my admiration for my students' tenacity on a recent and very tentative date with my former girlfriend. She laughed and asked why I didn't just give them a sensible template. If you don't, she said, they're just going to find something worse online, right?

She was right, and I was glad to tell her so.

THE HUMBLE ESSAY AS A PRODUCT

So, tenacious student writers, the real answer to your question about what I and all your professors are looking for is first of all for you to become engaged in a thoughtful writing process. We want you to see how it works to think like we do within our various disciplines. Second, we are looking for your paper to look like your answer to a good question and to fit within the presentation guidelines for our various disciplines. That's the real answer.

However, if you really want a template, then try this:

The Opening: Begin the essay with a single paragraph that does the following, in this order:

1. Engages your readers in a sentence or two, and doesn't overdo it.

2. Introduces your general topic and then your narrower focus within that topic.

3. Introduces your question about this narrower focus.

4. States your answer to that question (optional, unless your professor expects it).

5. States the major divisions of the paper, in order, if your paper is four pages or longer.

The Body: Use about 80 percent of your essay to explain

and defend your answer to the question. The body should use paragraphs to divide the explanations, evidence, and reasons into manageable blocks of text.

It does the following, in this order:

1. Defines the key terms of your answer, probably.

2. Explains your answer clearly, using examples as needed and, together with any definitions, doesn't take up more than a quarter of the body.

3. Defends your answer with the direct evidence and/or reasons that have led you to accept this answer as the best available answer, organizing your defense according to internal or other logical patterns and making those clear to readers with topic sentences and transitions.

4. Considers and responds to alternative views and evidence with respect and honesty, but doesn't spend more than a quarter of the body doing so.

The Closing: End the paper with a paragraph or two (or more for scientific papers — ask your science professors what *they're* looking for) that pulls the entire paper together. Take your time with this.

Your closing does the following, in this order:

1. Summarizes the key points of your defense.

2. Summarizes your response to any alternative views that you've considered.

3. Restates your answer to the question with more precision than in the opening, underscoring the importance of this idea within the context of this topic.

4. Encourages your readers to do something with the idea, but only if reasonable for the assignment or situation.

THE ACTUAL MEANING OF "ESSAY"

There's one final thing you should know about the college essay. The word "essay" means, in so many words, "to fart around." Go ahead and look it up. They're too embarrassed to use the actual phrase in a dictionary, but it's implied. This is something they don't teach you in high school for obvious reasons. It's something we don't teach you in college because we're so serious here. Even so, it's true, and I'll prove it to you.

Let's go back to your professors and the reason they assign essays in the first place. They don't assign essays for their own benefit. They don't even assign them because they care about you personally — they barely know you. No, they only assign essays — at no small personal cost to themselves — because they want you to enjoy their disciplines the way they do. Writing an essay is your chance to play at being a professor.

And what do professors do when they're not teaching? They fart around! They read what they feel like reading. They follow their curiosity. They snoop around libraries and field stations. They check out what their enemies have written lately and make plans to undo their enemies with even smarter essays of their own. They let their minds wander. They come up with all sorts of interesting questions and then poke around looking for ways to answer them. By assigning that essay, they've essentially said, "Join me. This is cool."

So join them already. It really *is* cool.

Don't write an essay about something you already know just because it's easy and you can do it. That's not farting around. Don't recycle old work you've turned in for other classes. And for the love of all things academic and good, don't download or buy an essay and pass it off as your own work. When you do any of the above, you don't learn anything worthwhile, and you certainly don't develop an appreciation for what it means to fart around within that discipline. What a waste of tuition! What a waste of time!

Do you find the assignment boring? That's not the assignment's fault. Boring is as boring does. The assignment knows exactly how much fun it could be if you would just use your imagination and for five minutes stop asking what the professor is looking for. Fart around with that topic! Take a closer look and let yourself wonder about it until you find a question that amuses you, a problem that makes you wonder about solutions, an idea you'd really like to test.

You must never run away from supposedly boring or difficult topics and beg to write about something you care about or already know about. College is here to stretch you into something much larger and more interesting than your current self, so you can count on assignments that require you to look at new topics about which you know little or nothing. That's a good thing. That's what you or your parents or *someone* is buying with all that tuition — new topics, new ideas, a new version of you. Don't run away from that. Embrace it!

I know this can be painful sometimes, but at least try to have some fun. The fun really is out there and waiting for you and your imagination. If you rise to that challenge, if you make an honest effort to truly fart around, you will soon find out that there are no bad topics or boring assignments. There are only new opportunities for you and your imagination.